No Nonsense

FLY FISHING GUIDEBOOKS

Glenn Tinnin

Fly Fishing Arizona

A Quick, Clear Understanding of
Where to Fly Fish in Arizona

No Nonsense

FLY FISHING GUIDEBOOKS

Author
Glenn Tinnin

Maps, Illustrations & Production
Pete Chadwell, *Dynamic Arts*
Gary D. Smith, *Performance Design*

Front Cover Photo
Scott Baxter

Back Cover Photo
David Banks

Editors
Jim Yuskavitch & David Banks

Published By
No Nonsense Fly Fishing Guidebooks
P.O. Box 91858
Tucson AZ 85752-1858

Printed in USA

Disclaimer
While this guide will greatly help readers to fly fish, it is not a substitute for caution, good judgment and the services of a qualified fly fishing guide or outfitter.

No Nonsense Fly Fishing Guidebooks believes that in addition to local information and gear, fly fishers need clean water and healthy fish. The publisher encourages preservation, improvement, conservation, enjoyment and understanding of our waters and their inhabitants. A good way to do this is to support organizations dedicated to these ideas.

We are a member and sponsor of, and donor to The International Game Fish Association, Trout Unlimited, The Federation of Fly Fishers, Oregon Trout, California Trout, New Mexico Trout, Amigos Bravos, American Fly-Fishing Trade Association, American Rivers, Waterfowl U.S.A. and Ducks Unlimited. We encourage you to get involved, learn more and to join such organizations.

IGFA (954) 927-2628
Trout Unlimited (800) 834-2419
Federation of Fly Fishers (406) 585-7592
Oregon Trout (503) 222-9091
California Trout (415) 392-8887
New Mexico Trout (505) 344-6363
Amigos Bravos (505) 758-3874
A.F.F.T.A. (360) 636-0708
American Rivers (202) 347-7550
Ducks Unlimited (901) 758-3825

Acknowledgments

It takes the help of many knowledgeable people to write a book. The list of friends and others who gave me valuable information about fly fishing in Arizona nearly goes on forever.

Because I don't have the room to name everyone, I'll just list the ones I bugged the most. The following people gave me valuable information and many spent hours fishing with me. Special thanks to Darr Colburn, Dan Westfall, Al Harris, Terry Gunn, and Loren Bradley. Also, many thanks to the friends, relatives, and customers that I corralled into taking me to those out-of-the-way places just to test the waters.

Thanks to the many guides, fly shop owners and managers throughout the state who keep the fine sport of fly fishing alive and well in Arizona. Without their dedication, we would not have the angling opportunities that we now have. Among these folks are Dave and Barb Foster, Terry and Wendy Gunn, John Rohmer, Bob Willard, Rod McLeod, Jerry Jenkins, Victor Leibe, Loren and Debbie Bradley, Bob Polluck, and Jim Kirkman, as well as all the employees and guides that work out of the Arizona fly shops.

Wink Crigler, Gerald Scott, and Al Harris of the X-Diamond Ranch allowed my family, friends, and fly fishing school to take over the ranch on many occasions. I have used the ranch for much research, lots of fishing, and as a sanctuary for several years now. Thanks to the most hospitable people I know.

Thanks to David Banks, for the gentle nudges that kept me on track with this book. His direction and drive are most appreciated.

Lastly, I must thank the past and present staff at Complete Flyfishing for all their help while I researched and wrote this book. Thanks to Matt Baker, Craig Schumann, Maxeen Tinnin, Mike Adams, Rachel Connery, Jim Andras, Mike O'Connor, and Dillion Kennedy. I never would have been able to pull this book off without such a dedicated and helpful bunch.

Largemouth Bass

I would like to dedicate this book to Maxeen, my wife of over 20 years and my two sons, Cody, age 10, and Jamie, age 7. They have allowed me to pursue a career many only dream about. Without their understanding and support this book would not have come to fruition.

Fly Fishing in Arizona

Some thoughts on Regulations, Fish, & Water

Arizona is an expansive state. It seems that no matter where you happen to be, it's a long way to where you're going. Geologically, we have it all; deserts, high deserts, hill country, red rock canyons, the Grand Canyon, and several high elevation mountain ranges. Opportunity comes with this diversity. Where else can you comfortably go swimming in the morning and fly fishing for trout that afternoon. Or conclude a hard day at the office in downtown Phoenix by sipping a margarita while watching a Mexican sunset at Rocky Point?

To put all this in fishing perspective, we have some very good warm water fishing as well as excellent high mountain coldwater fishing. We have Lees Ferry and Lake Powell, one a cold water trout river, the other a warmwater bonanza, separated by a large dam. We have both high mountain trout streams and the rocky shoreline of the Sea of Cortez, only a 4½ hour drive from Phoenix. Just 30 minutes from anywhere in the city we can wet a line for warmwater fishes.

I know this may sound like a fairy tale, but it's one you can a be part of once you learn where all the good Arizona fishing waters are. That's why we published this guidebook.

We have many non-native fish including arctic grayling, walleye, pike, and tilapia that cruise around many of our lakes. The striped bass population has grown out of control in the lower Colorado drainage, as well as in Lake Powell. These planted fish eat everything they can and have wiped out populations of native fishes including some trout fisheries. Of course, the trout fisheries were created in the waters below the dams by the same Arizona Game & Fish Department that stocked stripers in those waters in the first place.

Another problem our Game & Fish Department has is keeping the thousands of anglers in this state happy. Everyone who buys a license wants to catch fish, and most of the fishing public wants to keep them. Enter put-and-take.

Our state's hatchery program is among the largest in the U.S. Arizona Game & Fish stocks millions of catchable fish in our lakes and streams annually. Many of these hatchery fish are stocked in healthy waters capable of maintaining wild trout populations—the number one species sought by the fly rodder.

With ongoing input from anglers this put-and-take mentality is beginning to change. Several fisheries have protective regulations, while several others are set aside for artificial fly and lure angling only. A couple of fisheries are catch and release showing that Arizona has just begun to recognize the value of wild fish.

Another problem that could affect the future of fly fishing in this state, as well as others, is the push by the federal government to protect native species. This has put Arizona fishers and our Game & Fish Department in a tough position. Almost all our gamefish are non-natives. Among our healthy wild trout populations only the Apache trout is indigenous to Arizona. The U.S. Fish and Wildlife Service has declared war on all non-native species of trout. In many places brown and rainbow trout have established self-reproducing wild populations and are in danger of being eradicated under current policies.

Many of the species the USFWS has targeted to bring back to health are not gamefish. These include the razorback sucker, flannelmouth sucker, several species of chub, and the Gila trout. The Gila has been extinct in Arizona for some time thanks to overstocking of non-native trout, and poor logging and cattle practices over the last 100 years.

Maybe this is good, maybe not, but I believe the public and not the politically controlled U.S. Fish and Wildlife Service or the state Game & Fish Department, should make that decision. So I suggest you do your homework on these issues, vote, and communicate with local and national wildlife departments. Join Trout Unlimited, the Federation of Fly Fishers, and other gamefish groups. This may be the only way to ensure the future of fishing for generations to come!

Contents

Arizona Vicinity Map

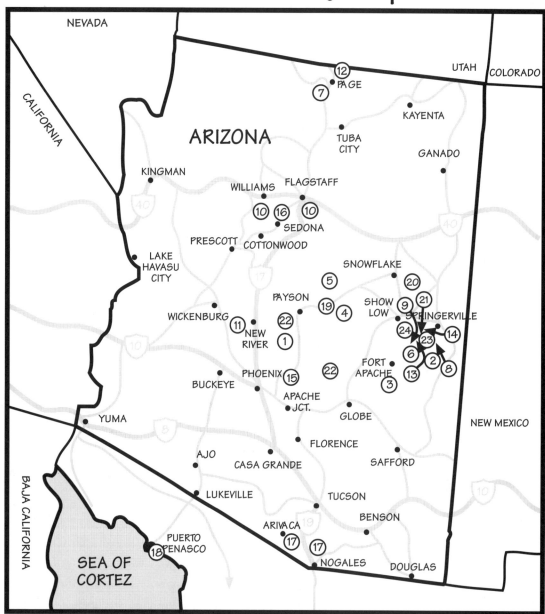

Referenced Streams, Lakes, and Reservoirs

1. Bartlett Lake
2. Black River, east and west forks
3. Black River, Reservation downstream
4. Canyon Creek
5. Chevelon Canyon Reservoir
6. Christmas Tree Lake
7. Colorado River (Lees Ferry)
8. Crescent Lake
9. Earl Park Lake
10. Lake Mary & J D Dam Lake
11. Lake Pleasant
12. Lake Powell
13. Lee Valley Reservoir
14. Little Colorado River
15. Lower Salt River
16. Oak Creek
17. Patagonia/Arivaca Lakes
18. Puerto Peñasco (Rocky Point)
19. Rim Country
20. Silver Creek
21. Sunrise Lake
22. Warm Water Lakes
23. White Mountain Lakes
24. White River, north fork

Conditions by the Month
Arizona Fly fishing

FEATURED WATERS	JANUARY	FEBRUARY	MARCH	APRIL	MAY	JUNE	JULY	AUGUST	SEPTEMBER	OCTOBER	NOVEMBER	DECEMBER
① Bartlett Lake												
② Black River, east and west forks			W									
③ Black River, Reservation downstream			W	W							W	
④ Canyon Creek												
⑤ Chevelon Canyon Reservoir			W	W							W	
⑥ Christmas Tree Lake												
⑦ Colorado River (Lees Ferry)			W	W							W	W
⑧ Crescent Lake			W	W							W	
⑨ Earl Park Lake			W	W							W	
⑩ Lake Mary & J D Dam Lake			W	W							W	
⑪ Lake Pleasant		W		W								
⑫ Lake Powell												
⑬ Lee Valley Lake			W	W							W	
⑭ Little Colorado River			W	W							W	
⑮ Lower Salt River												
⑯ Oak Creek			W	W							W	
⑰ Patagonia/Arivaca Lakes												
⑱ Puerto Peñasco (Rocky Point)			W									
⑲ Rim Country												
⑳ Silver Creek	W	W									W	W
㉑ Sunrise Lake			W									
㉒ Warm Water Lakes												
㉓ White Mountain Lakes			W	W							W	
㉔ White River, north fork			W	W							W	

FEATURED WATERS
① REFERS TO NUMBERS ON VICINITY MAP
BEST   GOOD   FAIR   POOR
CLOSED   W WEATHER DEPENDENT

The Arizona No Nonsense Fly-O-Matic
A Quick-Start Guide for Fly Fishing Arizona

Gamefish

Anglers find rainbow, brown, brook, cutthroat and Apache trout and arctic grayling in the state's cold waters. Warmer, low elevation waters hold largemouth, smallmouth, white and yellow bass as well as some striped bass, crappie, bluegill, pike, and walleye. It's also possible to catch carp, suckers, and catfish on a fly.

Catch and Release

Catch and release has become a way of life for most serious fly fishers. It's the best way to insure that fish grow larger and that good populations are maintained. It is especially important when fishing for wild trout. Over the years, many wild populations were stressed from overfishing and stocking.

When practicing catch and release, land the fish quickly! Over-stressing a fish can kill it, even after it is released. Use a rod capable of fighting and landing the fish in short order. It is NOT cool to fight a fish to exhaustion using a rod too small for the job! It IS cool to release a fish unharmed to fight again.

Use barbless hooks and, if a net is necessary, use one that has a soft cotton bag that will not scratch up the fish or wipe off its slime.

Weather

During the summer, the temperature in the desert may reach 120°. In the mountains in the winter temperatures may drop to 0°. Welcome to Arizona!

It's usually too cold to fish in the mountains in the winter. Most of the lakes freeze over and the roads leading to streams and rivers are closed. The exception is Lees Ferry, a tailrace fishery that maintains a constant water temperature of 48° to 52° year-round. The air temperature here is very cold. Dress in layers, with long underwear that wicks moisture away from the skin, a fleece or pile layer next for warmth, and a breathable waterproof, windproof layer on the outside.

Summers can be very warm, even in the mountains. Wear breathable layers that offer sun protection. Use lots of sunscreen and drink plenty of water.

Hazards & Safety

In mid- to late summer, be prepared for afternoon thunderstorms. It doesn't rain much in Arizona, but when it does, look out! We can get a whole lot of rain in a very short period. Flash floods are serious business here. Always be prepared and stay out of narrow canyons if the weather looks stormy.

Hypothermia can be a problem in the winter. Stay warm and dry and wear the right clothing. If you do fall in the water when the air temperature is 15, survival may depend on the thermal protection of your clothing, even when it is wet.

Arizona has rattlesnakes in the lower elevations. Watch your step and go around them. Don't wave a fly rod around during electrical storms; if you can see lightning, it's close enough to zap you.

Drink lots of water and apply lots of sunscreen. I recommend carrying a bottle of water and a tube of sfp 15+ at all times. Lots of Arizonans who don't get heat stroke or have skin cancer. For the same reason, wear a good hat and sunglasses at all times while fishing. The sunglasses also protect your eyes.

Warm Water Lakes

Lower elevation warmwater lakes are the places to go during the early spring while the streams are high, and late in the fall after the snow begins to fly in the high country. All these lakes fish well from a bass boat, float-tube or kick-boat. To catch bass on the surface use poppers; wigglebugs when the bass are chasing shad. Clouser Minnows work better when the fish are a little deeper. Terrestrials, such as grassHoppers, Damselflies and dragonflies work very well in the shallow coves that are prevalent on these lakes.

Cold Water Lakes

The mountain lakes provide very good fly fishing for trout in the warmer months. Float tubing these cool lakes is the perfect solution to the 100-plus days in the valley of the sun. The prolific damselfly hatch lasts well into summer and is the main fly used to catch fat and sassy lake-dwelling trout. These fish also hit Woolly Buggers and streamers as well as Hopper patterns and nymphs.

Small Streams

True fly fishing aficionado's will appreciate the many miles of high elevation trout streams in our White Mountains and Rim Country. Although some of this water is very small, one still finds good populations of trout feeding on Mayflies, stoneflies, and Caddisflies.

The name of the game here is stealth! Keep the following in mind: stay low, approach from downstream when possible, don't line the fish, don't wear white, and don't splash the water. Leaders should be long and tippets fine. If you're not catching fish in these waters, or are only catching small fish, re-read this paragraph.

The best technique is to fish a two-fly system. The upper fly should be a large dry fly like a Hopper. Tie on an 18-inch piece of 5X tippet and add a nymph to the tippet. The nymph is usually beaded to add weight. This can be a dynamite combination, but it takes a little getting used to.

Lees Ferry
One fishery in the state where I highly recommend hiring a guide, at least for the first visit, is Lees Ferry. The river is large and swift and the best fishing is as far as 15 miles up river. A boat with a motor large

enough to allow it to plane when loaded is absolutely necessary. The fishing is tricky at first. Take lots of split shot and some strike indicators. You need a perfect dead drift to fool the educated fish here.

Flies and Their Use
Frankly, we do not have many flying insects in this arid country. That's both good and bad. We don't have to carry mosquito repellent, but we also don't get the prolific insect hatches that are in all fly fishers' dreams. About the best we get in Arizona is a good Caddis hatch late in the day. Sometimes a sporadic Baetis hatch occurs if we're lucky enough to get some afternoon clouds. Most Arizona trout dine on subsurface nymphs and other underwater fare. They come to the surface when something really juicy and big floats by. That's good for us!

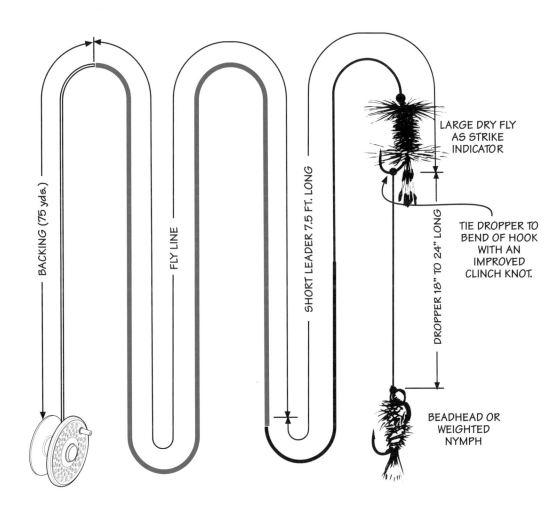

BACKING (75 yds.)

FLY LINE

SHORT LEADER 7.5 FT. LONG

LARGE DRY FLY AS STRIKE INDICATOR

TIE DROPPER TO BEND OF HOOK WITH AN IMPROVED CLINCH KNOT.

DROPPER 18" TO 24" LONG

BEADHEAD OR WEIGHTED NYMPH

Using a large dry fly as a strike indicator can be very effective in Arizona, Use the dry fly as you would a strike indicator, except that this "strike indicator" will hook a fish that rolls on it! Tie the dropper directly to the bend of the hook using an improved clinch knot.

On streams use a large dry fly, such as a #4 Stimulator or a #6 Madam X. If that doesn't get action, tie a #16 Beadhead Pheasant Tail about 18 inches below the dry and bingo! The flies that work the best on top are #8–#4 Stimulators, #10–#6 Madam Xs, #14–#18 Dave's Hoppers, #8–#4 Turck's Tarantulas, or big Chernobyl Ants. On the bottom use #14–#18 Beadhead Pheasant Tails and Hare's Ears, # 10–#16 Beadhead Caddis Larvae, or #12–#16 Yellow Sally Stonefly Nymphs. The double fly rigs used throughout the West work well also. Two dries—one large and one small—when the fish are eating very small dries, or two nymphs when the fish just will not come up for anything.

When a good hatch is on, just pick a fly that resembles the real bug. Make an agreeable presentation and drift and you'll have no problem hooking fish. The only true hatches we have that will get the fish on the surface are Caddis and Baetis hatches. Always have plenty of Elk Hair Caddis and Parachute Adams in your box. We also have some good action on Yellow Sally Stoneflies in the late summer.

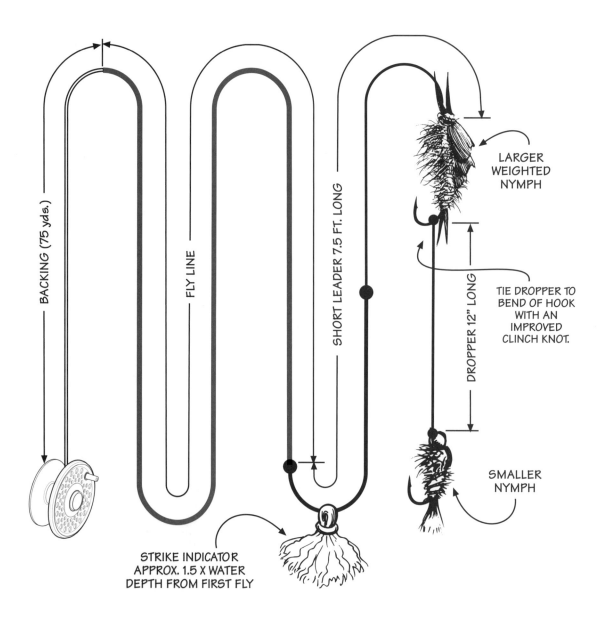

BACKING (75 yds.)

FLY LINE

SHORT LEADER 7.5 FT. LONG

LARGER WEIGHTED NYMPH

DROPPER 12" LONG

TIE DROPPER TO BEND OF HOOK WITH AN IMPROVED CLINCH KNOT.

SMALLER NYMPH

STRIKE INDICATOR APPROX. 1.5 X WATER DEPTH FROM FIRST FLY

Another popular two-fly rig for fly fishing in Arizona uses a typical strike indicator placed on the butt section of the leader roughly 1-½ times the water depth from the first fly. Use a large weighted nymph as the first fly, and then add a dropper and use a smaller nymph as a "trailer."

Rods

    Small streams, 3 or 4 wt., 6'–8'.
    Lees Ferry, 5 wt., 9'.
    Lakes, 6 wt., 9'.
    Bass and pike, 8 wt., 9'.

Reels

If you pursue dinky fish or bass, it doesn't really matter what reel you use. If the fish are going to pull any drag at all, a disc drag reel is best, especially if you're using a small tippet.

Line

Weight forward floating lines are the most popular and useful in Arizona. For small rods, a double taper line provides better dry fly presentation and roll casts. Use sinking lines for lakes. For bass, use an intermediate sinking line like the Stillwater Line manufactured by Scientific Anglers. A floating line is also useful for bass.

Wading Gear

The only places neoprene waders are mandatory in Arizona are Lees Ferry and in cold water lakes. Because a lot of our fishing is during the warmer months, I suggest breathable, chest-high waders. Also wear a felt-soled boot that offers good ankle support.

Private Fly fishing Waters

There are only one or two fisheries that are controlled by private landowners. Many stretches of stream in the state run near or through cattle leases on BLM lands. Treat these ranches as though private. Don't litter, don't drive off established roads, and leave gates as you found them. DON'T CLOSE AN OPEN GATE! It's open for a reason. Always close a gate that was closed when you found it. The only completely private fishery in Arizona that I know of, that is open to the public, is the X-Diamond Ranch.

Guides

USE 'EM! For the money, they are the best investment in fly fishing. The guide will not only show you where the fish are, but tell you what techniques and flies work best and coach you to a successful day.

Crowding

Crowding is generally not a problem in Arizona except at Lees Ferry in the easy to get to places. Fish areas that are a little harder to get to and chances are good you won't see anyone at all! Yes, you will have to walk for a few minutes.

Up to Date Information—Local Shops

Most fly fishing shops are more than happy to give you information. They can steer you to the better spots, tell you the local flies, give you directions and recommend a guide. Some shops have leases or use agreements on private property. Go to the shops and ask questions!

Ratings

Of course, a rating system will vary from state to state and from rater to rater. I have rated Arizona's waters from 1, being the poorest to 10, being the best in relation to the others. I have also figured in the best fishing in the West as a place to start, hence no 10's in Arizona. Also, remember these ratings reflect my experience and the experience of several other pretty good fly fishers. A beginner will not have the luck a more experienced angler will and an experienced angler will not have the luck a guide will.

A 5 in this guidebook is worth fishing, but may not be good enough to fish very often. I will fish these waters, but only after other constraints prevent me from going somewhere better. A 7 is pretty good, a 9 is great for most of us, unless you're one of those spoiled types that only fish the holy waters of Montana. I reserve the 10 rating for those waters.

The No Nonsense Guide

I have tried to save your time and use only the words that get you the facts you need to fly fish Arizona. That's why I use these books for my own information and planning. I hope this book proves as useful in your pursuit of Arizona fish as others in this series have proven valuable for me.

    • *Abide by the laws*
    • *Respect property rights*
    • *Never crowd another fly fisher*
    • *Catch and Release*
    • *Carry out your litter*
    • *Support conservation*

Common Game Fish in Arizona

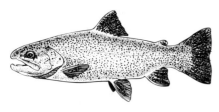

APACHE TROUT
Unique to the White Mountains of Arizona, apache trout have a dark green back, pale yellowish flanks and many very fine black spots.

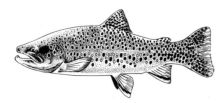

BROWN TROUT
Brown colored back with big black spots. A square tail and black and red spots on sides with light blue rings. Hard to catch, easily spooked.

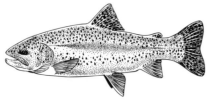

RAINBOW TROUT
The most abundant wild and hatchery fish. An olive-bluish back with small black spots. Sides have light red or pink band. Lake 'bows are often all silver.

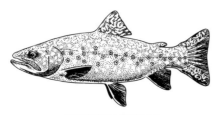

BROOK TROUT
Actually char (Dolly , Bull Trout, Lake Trout, etc.). Black, blue-gray or green back, mottled light colored markings. Sides have red spots with blue rings. Square tail. Lower fins red, striped with black and white. Prefers colder water.

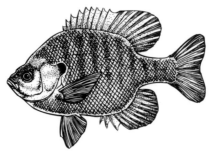

BLUEGILL
Mottled blue and green with orange or red breast. Large black spot on gill cover.

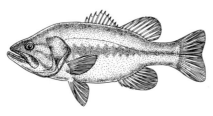

LARGEMOUTH BASS
Green back, silvery sides, large irregular spots. Deeply forked tail.

SMALLMOUTH BASS
Dark brown back with vertical bronze stripes on the sides. Spiny dorsal fin (9-10 spines) hasn't a deep notch separating the soft dorsal fin.

GRAYLING
In the whitefish family. Silvery gray with black spots. Very large dorsal fin spotted with blue and edged with pink. Ventral fins are striped with purple.

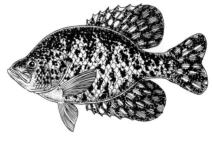

CRAPPIE
Silver, blueish or greenish with dark green or black splotches on the sides. Compressed body. Spines on dorsal, anal fins.

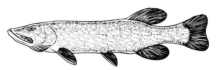

NORTHERN PIKE
Blueish to gray-green back with yellow to light gold spots in irregular rows. Long slender body, duck-billed snout and very sharp teeth.

STRIPED BASS
Greenish back, 7-8 horizontal stripes on silver background on sides. Spiny dorsal fin attached to soft dorsal. Longer than other bass.

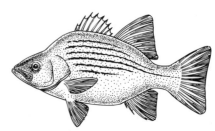

WHITE BASS
Similar to a striped bass, more silvery. Stripes less pronounced.

The Best Flies to Use in Arizona

TROUT

| ELK HAIR Caddis | ADAMS | PARACHUTE ADAMS | ROYAL WULFF | COMPARADUN | ARIZONA PEACOCK LADY |

| BURK'S ADULT DAMSEL | DAVE'S HOPPER | STIMULATOR | MADAM X | SCHROEDER'S PARA-HOPPER |

| TURCK'S TARANTULA | KAUFMANN'S STONE | BEAD HEAD HARE'S EAR | BEAD HEAD PHEASANT TAIL | BEAD HEAD PRINCE |

| SOFT HACKLE PHEASANT TAIL | BEAD HEAD LATEX CADDIS LARVA | BOB'S MARABOU DAMSEL | WOOLLY BUGGER | MUDDLER MINNOW |

BASS

| LEFTY'S DECEIVER | PENCIL POPPER | CLOUSER MINNOW |

| DAHLBERG DIVER | DAVE'S CRAYFISH | SWIMMING FROG |

| WHITLOCK'S DEER HAIR POPPER | WIGGLE BUG | DEER HAIR MOUSE/RAT |

Arizona's Apache Trout

Top Arizona
Fly Fishing Waters

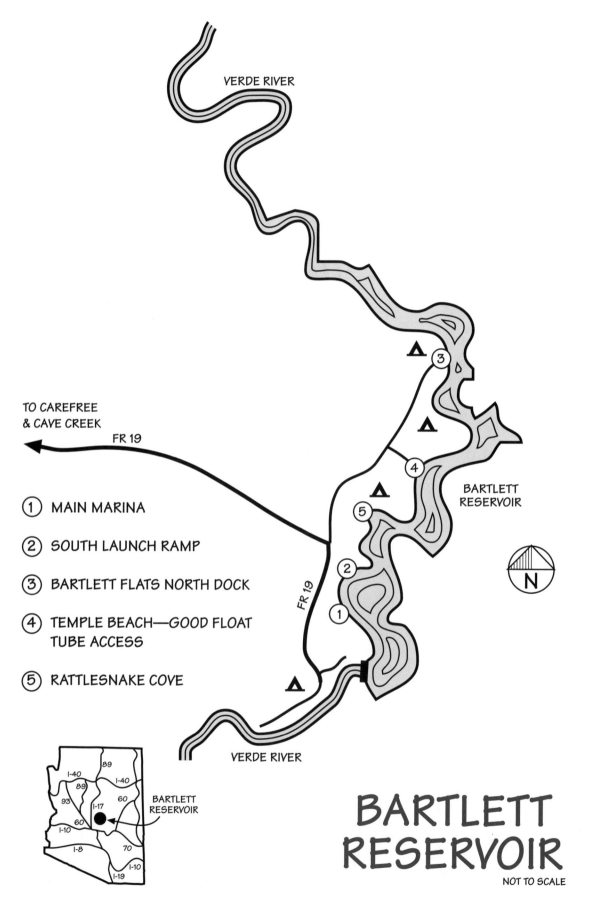

VERDE RIVER

TO CAREFREE
& CAVE CREEK

FR 19

① MAIN MARINA

② SOUTH LAUNCH RAMP

③ BARTLETT FLATS NORTH DOCK

④ TEMPLE BEACH—GOOD FLOAT
TUBE ACCESS

⑤ RATTLESNAKE COVE

FR 19

BARTLETT
RESERVOIR

N

VERDE RIVER

I-40 89
I-40
89 60
93 I-17
60 BARTLETT
RESERVOIR
I-10
I-8 70
I-10
I-19

BARTLETT
RESERVOIR

NOT TO SCALE

Bartlett Reservoir

Bass fishing with a fly rod is just beginning to catch on in Arizona and Bartlett Reservoir, located in a canyon just a 20 minute drive from Scottsdale, is a great place to partake. The lake sports lots of smallmouth and largemouth bass as well as some crappie and bluegill. It takes good casting and a powerful hook set, but when a bass takes your fly on the surface, the experience is explosive.

Amidst cacti and other desert plants, this low elevation lake is 2,815 acres, has 33 miles of shoreline and is up to 188 feet deep in places. Your best bet is to fish the coves, which are easy to reach from shore, or by kick boat. You'll do better casting from a motorboat into brushy areas near downed trees and bushes. Floating and sinking lines work well with Clouser Minnows and Woolly Buggers. The lake can be busy with water and jet skiers on some days. Start fishing early in the morning to avoid the crowds.

To get to Bartlett from Scottsdale take Scottsdale Road north to Cave Creek Road to FR 205 (Horseshoe Dam Road), which turns into FR 19. To get to the lake via I-17, take Exit 223 (Carefree Hwy.) to Cave Creek Road and follow the signs.

WIGGLE BUG

CLOUSER MINNOW DEEP

Types of Fish
Largemouth and smallmouth bass, crappie, pike, sunfish.

Known Hatches & Baitfish
Threadfin shad, crayfish, grasshoppers.

Equipment to Use
Rods: 6 to 8 weight, 9'.
Line: Floating, sinking, sink tip.
Leaders: Floating lines, 6' to 9' tapered to 10 lb. Sinking lines, 3' tapered to 8 to 10 lb.
Wading or Boating: Best from a motorboat, but a float tube or kick-boat will do. Hip boots or lightweight waders around the edges.

Flies to Use
Top water: Popper, Diver, Wiggle-bug, Hopper, Damselfly, Dragonfly.
Sub-surface: Water-pup, Clouser Minnow, Deceiver, Water-snake, Woolly Buggers.

When to Fish
Spring and fall, early morning. Late afternoon in summer.

Seasons & Limits
Fish year-round. The limits and regulations change so consult the state regulations.

Accommodations & Services
Convenience store at the lake. Carefree and Cave Creek are close and have all services.

Nearby Fly Fishing
Smallmouth bass in the Verde River above the lake.

Rating
Very busy most of the time and it can be pretty hot, a 6.

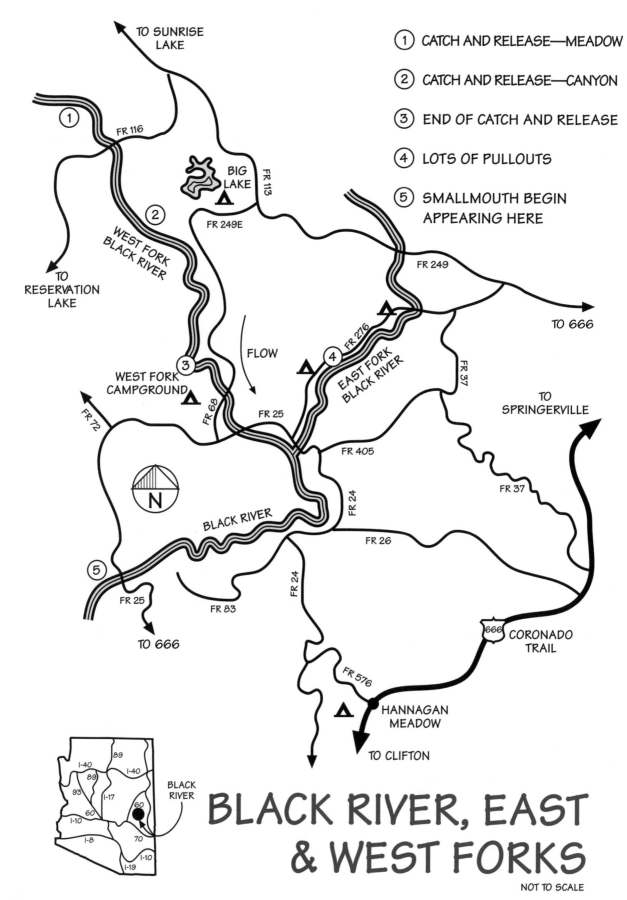

1. CATCH AND RELEASE—MEADOW
2. CATCH AND RELEASE—CANYON
3. END OF CATCH AND RELEASE
4. LOTS OF PULLOUTS
5. SMALLMOUTH BEGIN APPEARING HERE

TO SUNRISE LAKE
FR 116
BIG LAKE
FR 113
FR 249E
WEST FORK BLACK RIVER
TO RESERVATION LAKE
FR 249
TO 666
FLOW
FR 276
EAST FORK BLACK RIVER
FR 37
WEST FORK CAMPGROUND
FR 68
FR 25
TO SPRINGERVILLE
FR 72
FR 405
FR 24
FR 37
N
BLACK RIVER
FR 26
TO 666
FR 25
FR 83
FR 24
666 CORONADO TRAIL
FR 576
HANNAGAN MEADOW
TO CLIFTON

BLACK RIVER
I-40   89
I-40
89
93   I-17
60   60
I-10
I-8   70
I-10
I-19

BLACK RIVER, EAST & WEST FORKS

NOT TO SCALE

22

The Black River
East and West Forks

The East and West Forks of the Black River are two of the most popular and productive flywaters in the state. They're in the alpine zone of the White Mountains in Arizona that are reminiscent of the Colorado High Country.

The East Fork is popular and you will have trouble finding solitude. It is worth a visit, but to avoid the crowds, go in the early spring and late fall. The West Fork is just the opposite. A dusty, dirt road leads to the only access on the upper creek, which is where most fly fishers go. A large portion of the stream is high in the mountains. There is good brown trout fishing below the barriers which is still in the catch and release area. The West Fork should be an above average fishery for some time to come!

Both streams flow clear and low throughout the summer and fall. The many riffles, pools and runs are perfect for the small stream angler. The West Fork is one of only two streams in Arizona designated catch and release. It is also full of Apache trout.

Small Caddis and mayfly imitations work well during the summer, but you'll have the best success with big grasshopper imitations. The most productive technique is to use a Hopper, Caddis or Stonefly dry with a nymph tied on as a dropper.

Access to the East Fork or lower West Fork is via Hwy. 666, from Hannagan Meadow or Alpine. Access to the West Fork is easiest from the North, past Sunrise Lake to Forest Service Road 116.

Types of Fish
West Fork, upper catch and release section, Apache trout. Lower West Fork and East Fork, rainbow and brown trout.

Known Hatches
Baetis, caddis, golden and brown stoneflies, yellow sally.

Equipment to Use
Rods: 3 to 5 weight, 7-½' to 9'.
Line: Floating double taper, since most fishing is in close.
Leaders: 5X, 7-½'.
Wading: Wade both rivers in hip boots or lightweight waders.

Flies to Use
Dries: #10–18 Adams, #16–20 Baetis, Blue Winged Olive, #12–16 Tan Caddis, Yellow Stimulators, #6–14 Golden and Brown Stoneflies, #4–6 Big Hoppers, Madam X.
Nymphs: Gold Ribbed Hare's Ear, Pheasant Tail, Stonefly, Caddis pupae.

When to Fish
Spring, summer, fall.

Seasons & Limits
West Fork is catch and release on 11 mile section from confluence of Hayground Creek to the White Mountain Apache Indian Reservation boundary. Limits on East Fork change. Check Arizona regulations.

Accommodations & Services
Lots of camping along the East Fork. Closest camping to the West Fork is at Big Lake or Winn campgrounds. Hotel at Sunrise Lake. The closest town is Greer.

Nearby Fly Fishing
Lee Valley Reservoir, Reservation Lake, Crescent Lake, Big Lake, Little Colorado River.

Rating
The West Fork is a solid 8, at least for now. As the fish get larger it may become crowded. The East Fork a 5, due to put-and-take management and crowding.

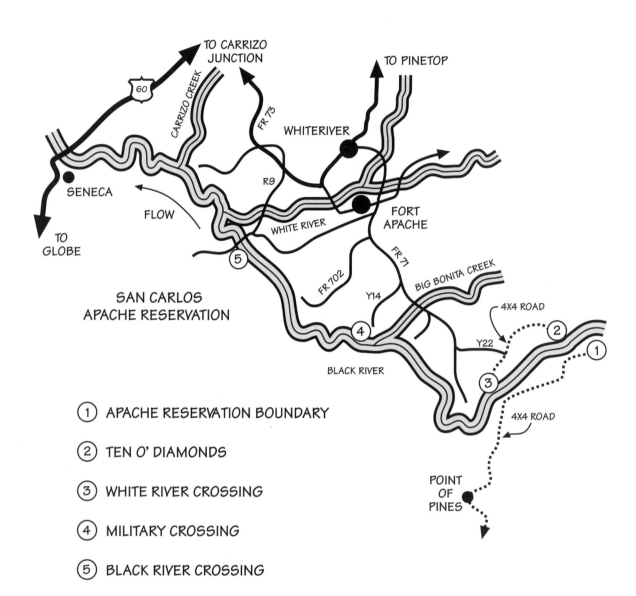

TO CARRIZO
JUNCTION

TO PINETOP

60

CARRIZO CREEK

FR 73

WHITERIVER

SENECA

R9

FLOW

WHITE RIVER

FORT
APACHE

TO
GLOBE

FR 71

BIG BONITA CREEK

FR 702

Y14

4X4 ROAD

SAN CARLOS
APACHE RESERVATION

Y22

2

1

5

4

3

BLACK RIVER

4X4 ROAD

① APACHE RESERVATION BOUNDARY

② TEN O' DIAMONDS

③ WHITE RIVER CROSSING

④ MILITARY CROSSING

⑤ BLACK RIVER CROSSING

POINT
OF
PINES

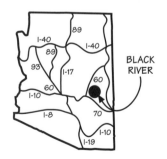

BLACK
RIVER

I-40   89

I-40

89

93

I-17

60

I-10

60

I-8

70

I-10

I-19

N

BLACK RIVER

NOT TO SCALE

Black River

Reservation downstream to the Salt River

The longest, high-quality fishing river in the state, the Black would take many summers to explore fully. The area is famous for its bad roads, four-wheeling, and true wilderness. If you're up to the challenge of driving bumpy dirt access roads, you'll be rewarded with outstanding fly fishing.

The Black's headwaters begin near 7,500' in elevation, making it a true Arizona coldwater fishery. Its upper reaches are cloaked in pines and firs, while scrub oak and cottonwoods line the lower river. Although much of the river flows through deep canyons it's mostly low gradient with slow-flowing pools. This makes for easy wading in most places.

Fishing for smallmouth bass attracts most anglers to the lower river, where they use Woolly Buggers and Muddler Minnows. Small nymphs also work as do hopper patterns on the surface. You'll find brown and rainbow trout on the upper river.

There are many access points for the upper and lower stretches. The better fishing in the upper region is northwest of Hannagan Meadow and southwest from Big Lake. This is where the Black becomes the boundary between the Fort Apache and San Carlos Indian Reservations. These areas are accessed from either reservation, depending on your final destination.

DAVE'S CRAYFISH

Types of Fish
Brown and rainbow trout, smallmouth bass.

Known Hatches & Baitfish
Sculpin, minnows, and tons of crayfish. caddisflies, stoneflies, Baetis mayflies in the upper trout water.

Equipment to Use
Rods: 3 to 6 weight, 7-½' to 9'.
Line: Floating and sink tip.
Leaders: 3X to 5X, 9'.
Wading: Chest-high neoprene waders and felt-soled boots. Can fish from a boat in the spring.

Flies to Use
Dries: Hoppers and other terrestrials, Elk Hair Caddis, Adams.
Nymphs: Prince, Hare's Ears, Pheasant Tail.
Streamers/Poppers: Woolly Buggers, Black Nosed Dace. Crayfish patterns and Clouser Minnows.

When to Fish
Best fishing is early spring and late fall. Avoid the rainy season in mid to late summer. Summer temperatures can exceed 100°.

Seasons & Limits
Year-round season. Limits change from year to year, but generally are high. Check current regulations.

Accommodations & Services
Whiteriver to the north and Point of Pines to the south have gas, stores, and other services. Primitive campsites are available along the river.

Nearby Fly Fishing
To the north and east are the best mountain stream trout fishing in the state.

Rating
There is lots of elbow room and the fishing is generally good, overall a 7.

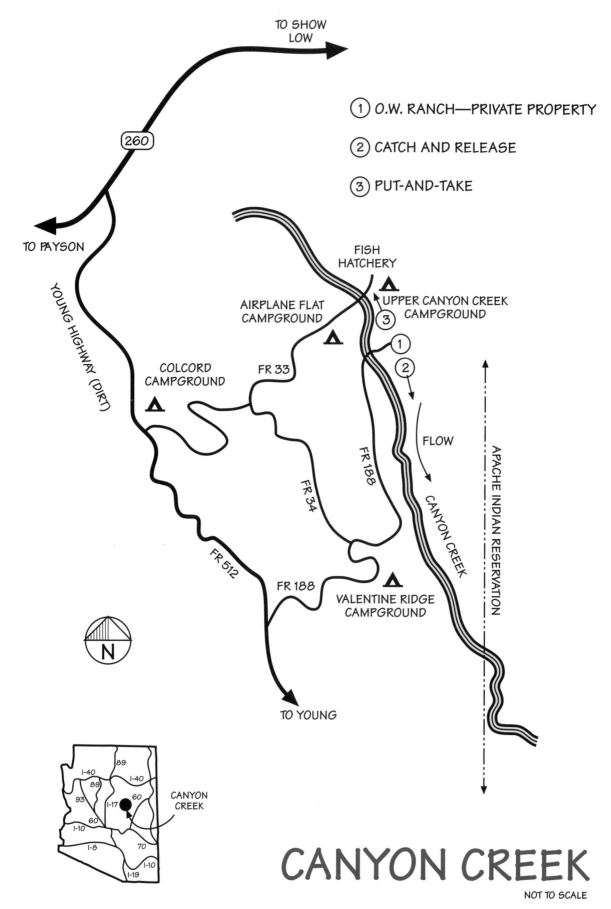

TO SHOW LOW

① O.W. RANCH—PRIVATE PROPERTY

② CATCH AND RELEASE

③ PUT-AND-TAKE

260

TO PAYSON

FISH HATCHERY

YOUNG HIGHWAY (DIRT)

AIRPLANE FLAT CAMPGROUND

UPPER CANYON CREEK CAMPGROUND

③

COLCORD CAMPGROUND

FR 33

①

②

FR 188

FLOW

FR 34

CANYON CREEK

APACHE INDIAN RESERVATION

FR 512

FR 188

VALENTINE RIDGE CAMPGROUND

N

TO YOUNG

I-40   89
I-40
89   60
93   I-17
60
I-10   70
I-8   I-10
I-19

CANYON CREEK

CANYON CREEK

NOT TO SCALE

Canyon Creek

During the summer of 2002 a forest fire swept through the lower sections of Canyon Creek, destroying the large trees and grasses and killing most if not all of the trout that lived there. A biologist as well as most of the anglers I have talked to estimate that the stream will come back, but it will take at least two to three years.

The uppermost section above the O.W. Ranch still fishes pretty darn well. It has a rainbow trout hatchery for put-and-take fishing. Only 2-½ hours from Phoenix and Scottsdale, Canyon Creek is a good day trip from the big city. The creek flows through some of the prettiest wildlife country in the state.

Once the river recovers, serious fly fishers should head for the O.W. Ranch section, where the water tends to be low and clear throughout the summer. This increases the challenge of hooking a big brown. Fishing with dry flies in the early morning or late afternoon is the most common tactic. A nymph with a dry fly as an indicator is also effective.

Because the creek is near the city, in summer the Forest Service campgrounds are filled with Boy Scouts and church groups. They usually stay on the upper river.

To reach Canyon Creek take Hwy. 87 (Beeline Hwy.) from Fountain Hills or Mesa to Payson. From Payson take Hwy. 260 east to the Young/Heber Hwy. The road turns to dirt at FR 512. Turn left at FR 33, at the primitive campground, and drive to the fork in the road. The right fork goes to the catch and release O.W. Ranch section. The left fork goes to the campgrounds, hatchery, and put-and-take water.

Types of Fish
Brown trout in the lower river, if it recovers, stocked rainbow and some brown trout in the baitfishing area.

Known Hatches
Good Baetis hatches in the spring and summer. Lots of grasshoppers in the warmer months. Sporadic hatches of golden stones. Some of the smallest black caddis hatches I've ever seen.

Equipment to Use
Rods: 3 to 4 weight, 7-½'. Smaller rods work when not windy.
Line: Double taper or floating.
Leaders: 5X, 6' to 9'.
Wading: Very shallow, hippers OK. Most locals wet-wade.

Flies to Use
Dries: Para Baetis, Para Adams, Hoppers, Stimulators, Elk Hair Caddis.
Nymphs: Hare's Ears, Pheasant Tails, Caddis Larvae and their Beadhead counterparts.
Streamers: Woolly Buggers.

When to Fish
Early spring through late fall. There is substantial runoff from the rim in the spring and lots of snow in the winter, making access nearly impossible.

Seasons & Limits
Spring through fall. Catch and release in the O.W. Ranch area. The limits in the upper creeks and baitfishing area change, so consult current regulations.

Accommodations & Services
About an hour from Payson. Closer to the small town of Christopher Creek.

Nearby Fly Fishing
The Rim Lakes, Willow Springs, and Black Canyon.

Rating
Upper 7, lower 0 for now but coming back; will probably be a 6 due to crowding and somewhat marginal water conditions.

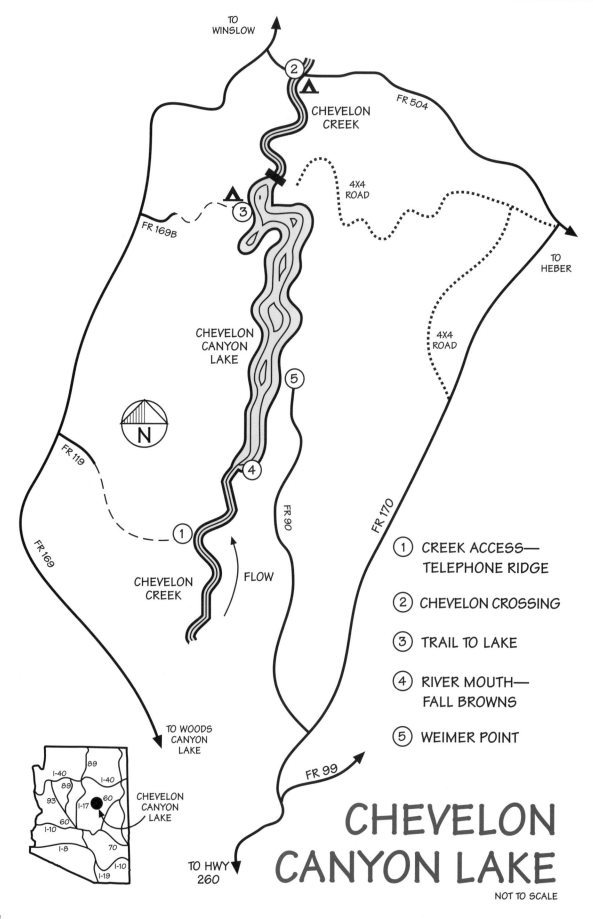

TO
WINSLOW

CHEVELON
CREEK

FR 504

4X4
ROAD

FR 169B

TO
HEBER

CHEVELON
CANYON
LAKE

4X4
ROAD

N

FR 119

FR 169

FR 90

FR 170

CHEVELON
CREEK

FLOW

① CREEK ACCESS—
TELEPHONE RIDGE

② CHEVELON CROSSING

③ TRAIL TO LAKE

④ RIVER MOUTH—
FALL BROWNS

⑤ WEIMER POINT

TO WOODS
CANYON
LAKE

FR 99

I-40   89
I-40
89
93   60
I-17
60
I-10
I-8   70
I-10
I-19

CHEVELON
CANYON
LAKE

TO HWY
260

CHEVELON
CANYON LAKE

NOT TO SCALE

Chevelon Canyon Lake

Many consider Chevelon Canyon Lake to be the best place in the state to fly fish for big browns. Its remote setting, at 6,400' in the Sitgreaves National Forest, combined with the steep hike down to the water, deter all but the most adventurous. This makes Chevelon the perfect place to search out big browns and rainbows.

With six miles of shoreline, this 200-acre lake is large by Arizona standards. Although shore access is unlimited, a float tube or kick boat is worth packing in because it will help you cover most of the water. A deep sinking line with a Woolly Bugger or Leech pattern is very effective here. Big Hoppers cast near shore also work well.

As of this writing, the Forest Service is planning a camping area near the lake that may also improve access. On the other hand, this might detract from the wilderness experience and encourage more visitors and anglers. It's best to fish Chevelon now.

To get to Chevelon Canyon Lake from Payson, take Hwy. 260 to FR 300 (Woods Canyon Lake turnoff), then 169 and 169B to the parking area. This is a 23-mile trip on gravel and dirt roads. The roads aren't maintained in the winter, and the Forest Service closes several gates to keep them from becoming rutted after the snow begins to fly.

TURCK'S
TARANTULA

WOOLLY BUGGER

Types of Fish
Brown and rainbow trout.

Known Hatches
Cicadas, callibaetis, Baetis mayflies, midges, maddis and lots of crayfish. Damselflies in the summer.

Equipment to Use
Rods: 5 to 6 weight, 9'.
Line: Floating or sinking.
Leaders: For floating, 5X, 9'. For sinking 3X, 3'.
Wading: A kick boat or float tube works very well here. Use chest-high waders and boots or fins.

Flies to Use
Dries: Any big dry to represent a Cicada. Para-Adams, Hoppers and adult Damselflies.
Nymphs: Pheasant Tails, Hare's Ears, Damselfly.
Streamers: Woolly Buggers, Leech imitations, Crayfish imitations.

When to Fish
Spring or fall.

Seasons & Limits
Year-round except during snow season. Limits change, so check current regulations.

Accommodations & Service
Woods Canyon Lake has a small store.

Nearby Fly Fishing
Woods Canyon Lake, Willow Springs Lake.

Rating
Remote with a lot of big fish, an 8.

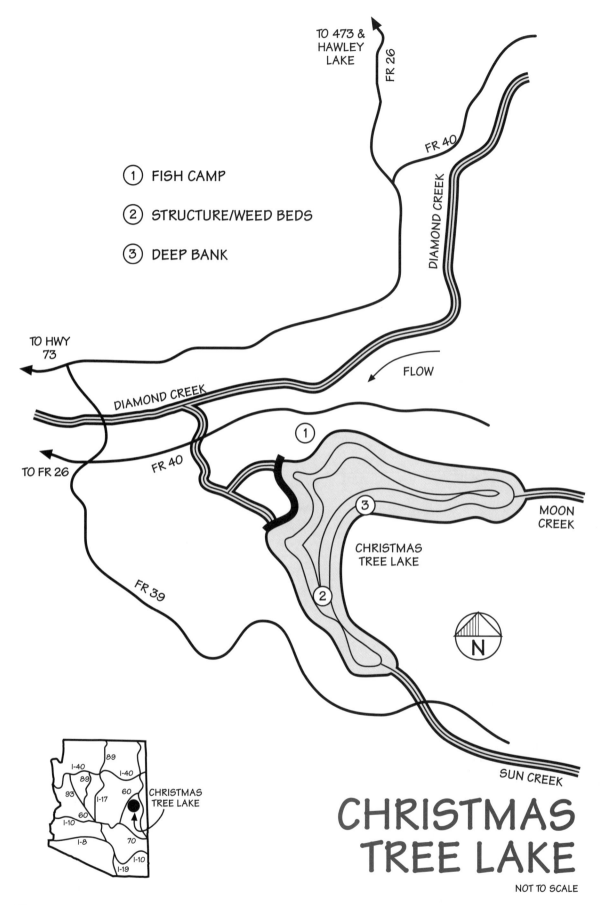

① FISH CAMP

② STRUCTURE/WEED BEDS

③ DEEP BANK

TO 473 &
HAWLEY
LAKE

FR 26

FR 40

DIAMOND CREEK

TO HWY
73

FLOW

DIAMOND CREEK

TO FR 26

FR 40

①

③

MOON
CREEK

CHRISTMAS
TREE LAKE

②

FR 39

N

SUN CREEK

CHRISTMAS
TREE LAKE

NOT TO SCALE

I-40
89
I-40
89
60
93
I-17
CHRISTMAS
TREE LAKE
60
I-10
I-8
70
I-10
I-19

Christmas Tree Lake

Reservations required! Like a good restaurant, this lake can be unforgettable. The world record Apache trout was taken here. The lake is limited to 20 anglers per day. Add the sheer beauty of the alpine setting and a wilderness camp complete with wall tents and cooks, and you have a world-class destination.

Most people describe this lake as being in the middle of nowhere. Travel the 20 or so minutes down a well-worn, and sometimes very rutted, dirt road and you'll probably agree. Once you arrive, this horseshoe-shaped, 41-acre paradise beckons the fly fisher to explore. Anglers playfully refer to Christmas Tree Lake as an Apache trout hatchery because of the many fish caught in the two- to five-pound range.

Christmas Tree is a float tube heaven with lots of nooks and crannies that need to be fished from a tube or boat. The Apache Game & Fish Department has small boats equipped with electric motors available, but the fly fisher is better off with the control of swim fins.

Many anglers catch fish just by dragging a fly around behind their float tube as they kick slowly. A better method is to locate and work likely looking holding areas by casting and slowly retrieving your fly.

The best spots are around downed trees and along the weed beds that form in early summer. Deep sinking lines are handy when the fish are deep (the lake is 42' deep in some places). Be prepared with a fast-sinking line.

To get to Christmas Tree Lake from the Phoenix area, take Hwy. 60 (or others) east to Hwy. 260. Take the Hawley Lake turnoff to State Rte. 473 and follow the signs. Trust these signs, as you'll swear you are lost!

Types of Fish
Apache, brown, and rainbow trout.

Known Hatches & Baitfish
Lots of damselflies, callibaetis, Baetis, and crayfish.

Equipment to Use
Rods: 5 to 6 weight, 9'.
Reels: A good disc drag reel.
Line: Floating and sinking.
Leaders: 5X, 9' for floating line, 3X, 3 to 4' for sinking line.
Wading: Best fished from a boat or float tube. Bring waders and fins.

Flies to Use
Dries: Adult Damsel, Adams, Hopper and Ant.
Nymphs: Damsels, Pheasant Tail, Hare's Ears.
Streamers: Woolly Buggers, Leeches.

When to Fish
Spring, summer, fall.

Seasons & Limits
Anglers must have a special use permit from the White Mountain Apache Tribe. Limit 20 anglers per day. Apache trout limit is one, 16" or longer. Brown trout limit is five. No limit on rainbows. Limits change, so be sure to check current regulations.

Accommodations & Services
In 1997 Apache Game & Fish established a fish camp complete with tents, toilets, and a kitchen. After the camp dates, camping is not permitted. The closest store is at Hawley Lake.

Nearby Fly Fishing
Near Earl Park Lake, Hawley Lake, and several nice small streams.

Rating
The best fly fishing lake in the state, a 9.

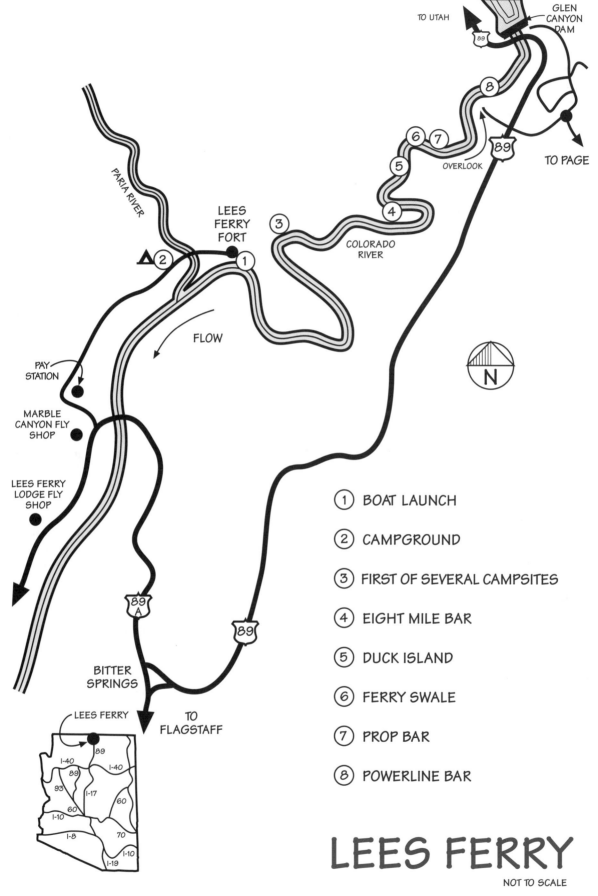

TO UTAH

GLEN CANYON DAM

89

8

6 7

5

OVERLOOK

89

TO PAGE

PARIA RIVER

LEES FERRY FORT

3

4

COLORADO RIVER

1

2

N

FLOW

PAY STATION

MARBLE CANYON FLY SHOP

LEES FERRY LODGE FLY SHOP

① BOAT LAUNCH

② CAMPGROUND

③ FIRST OF SEVERAL CAMPSITES

④ EIGHT MILE BAR

⑤ DUCK ISLAND

⑥ FERRY SWALE

⑦ PROP BAR

⑧ POWERLINE BAR

89 A

89

BITTER SPRINGS

TO FLAGSTAFF

LEES FERRY

89

I-40

I-40

89

93

I-17

60

60

I-10

I-8

70

I-10

I-19

LEES FERRY

NOT TO SCALE

Colorado River

Lees Ferry

This famous section of river is a true trophy trout fishery and one of the most spectacular places to fish in North America. Located at the entrance to the Grand Canyon in the high northern Arizona desert, the canyon's 1,000' sandstone cliffs are beautifully reflected in the Colorado River. This water runs clear 360 days a year. Only during the worst thunderstorm does the river cloud, and then only for a few hours.

The fish at the ferry average 12" to 14" but can grow over 20". They are fat and feisty and are taken on a number of wet and dry flies. An average day yields 10 to 20 nice fish. A good angler in the right place at the right time may have a 50-fish day.

A motorboat must be used to access the upper 15 miles of water from the boat launch at the Grand Canyon boundary to Glen Canyon Dam. Fishing is usually done while wading one of the many gravel bars. Sometimes drift fishing from a boat works well. The back eddies are usually fished from the boat. These eddies hold good numbers of large fish that key on Midges.

Most fish are taken using the classic dead drift nymphing technique. Rig a double-fly setup using a Scud and Midge pupae. Sometimes, in the shallowest water, use a large dry fly like a Stimulator with a Midge or Scud trailing on the Dropper. Woolly Buggers fished across and downstream also work well. Recently, Cicada and Hopper patterns have been good.

There are few biting insects in the area except mosquitoes during extremely wet years. You do need sunscreen, in winter and summer, as the sun is bright and temperatures are extreme. Highs push 120° in the summer and drop to 8–10° in the winter. Having clothing appropriate for prevailing conditions is important.

To reach Lees Ferry from Phoenix, go north through Flagstaff on Hwy. 89 and take the Hwy. 89A turnoff at Bitter Springs. The Marble Canyon bridge signals the turnoff is near. Turn down Lees Ferry Road and drive to the boat ramp at the end. To fish the walk-in area, park just beyond the small bridge that crosses the Paria River.

Types of Fish

Rainbow trout predominate. Cutthroat, brook and brown trout were stocked but are now rare.

Known Hatches & Baitfish

Gammerus scuds where there are aquatic plants, several species of midges. Rainbow fry are eaten by larger fish. The Game & Fish Department creates a feeding frenzy several times a year when they stock fingerlings.

Equipment to Use

Rods: 4 to 5 weight, 9'.
Reels: A good disc drag. Fish can take 100 yds. of line.
Line: WF floating, natural color in extremely clear water.
Leaders: 5X, 9'.
Wading: Chest-high waders, felt-soled boots, wading staff.

Flies to Use

Dries: Stimulator, Grasshopper, Unbelievable, floating Scud imitations, Midge patterns and clusters.
Nymphs: Pink, tan, or gray Scuds. Midge larvae and pupae, San Juan Worm.
Streamers: Black, brown, or olive Woolly Buggers.
.

When to Fish

Winter is best, when most trout spawn in the shallows. Spring and fall are good, as is summer, if you don't mind the heat.

Seasons & Limits

Fish year-round. Four fish under 12" can be kept. Artificial flies and lures only. Be sure to check current regulations as they change frequently.

Accommodations & Services

Marble Canyon Lodge has rooms, restaurant, gas, store, boat storage, laundry, and post office. Lees Ferry Lodge (three miles west) has rooms, two converted mobile homes, cafe, fly shop and boat rental. Cliff Dweller's Lodge (farther west) has about 20 rooms, gas station, and cafe.

Nearby Fly Fishing

Lake Powell has very good bass fishing in a picturesque setting. Utah and Colorado are not far. Most head to the San Juan River in New Mexico for more fly fishing.

Rating

Breathtaking beauty, crystal-clear water and year-round fishing. Because fish size is declining, a 7 or 8.

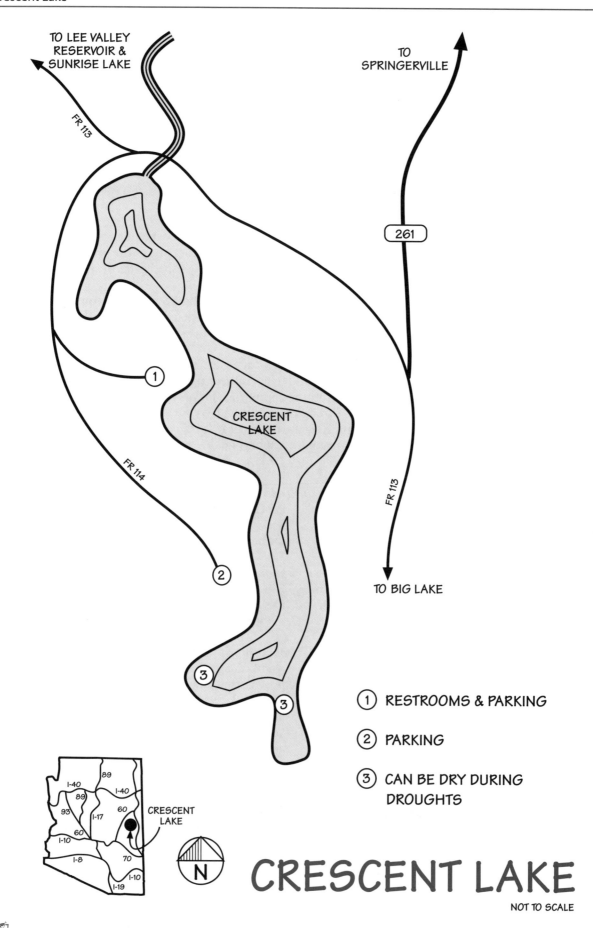

TO LEE VALLEY
RESERVOIR &
SUNRISE LAKE

FR 113

TO SPRINGERVILLE

261

CRESCENT
LAKE

FR 114

FR 113

TO BIG LAKE

1 RESTROOMS & PARKING

2 PARKING

3 CAN BE DRY DURING
DROUGHTS

CRESCENT LAKE

89
I-40
I-40
89
60
93
I-17
60
I-10
I-8
70
I-10
I-19

CRESCENT
LAKE

N

NOT TO SCALE

Crescent Lake

This easily accessible, crescent moon–shaped lake has long been a favorite destination for fly anglers going for rainbow and brown trout. A bonus, should Crescent not be fishing well, is the good fly fishing on other nearby streams and lakes. On the down side, this lake sometimes becomes crowded.

Though located in the White Mountains, the open prairie on which the lake lies can have strong winds that can hamper your casting. Otherwise Crescent is very fishable. A float tube or kick boat is a must.

Most of the lake is shallow, and weed beds form early in the season. Since this is where the trout hang out, fish the weeds and coves with sinking lines and nymphs. When a hatch is on, dry fly fishing can be good. Extreme ice-over and fish kill during very cold winters can slow spring fishing.

To get to Crescent Lake from the Phoenix area, take Hwy. 60 east (or any other Hwy. that goes to the mountains). Take FR 113 from Sunrise Lake or State Route 261 from Hwy. 260. The lake is right along the road.

BURK'S ADULT
DAMSEL

DAVE'S HOPPER

Types of Fish
Rainbow and brown trout.

Known Hatches & Baitfish
Damselflies, callibaetis, Baetis, crayfish, grasshoppers.

Equipment to Use
Rods: 6 weight, 9'.
Line: Sinking, sink tip, or floating.
Leaders: 3' for sinking lines; 9' for floating line.
Wading: Best fished with kick boat or float tube. Bring chest-high waders and fins.

Flies to Use
Dries: Adult Damsel, Adams, Hopper, BWO.
Nymphs: Damsel, Pheasant Tail, Hare's Ears.
Streamers: Woolly Buggers, Black Nosed Dace, Muddler Minnows, Crayfish imitations.

When to Fish
Spring, summer, fall.

Seasons & Limits
Open year-round, but generally freezes by mid-winter. Bag limit, six trout. Check current regulations.

Accommodations & Services
Parking and restrooms at the lake. Services near Big and Sunrise Lakes.

Nearby Fly Fishing
Sunrise Lake, West Fork of the Black River, Sheeps Crossing.

Rating
Even though it is popular, a weak 6.

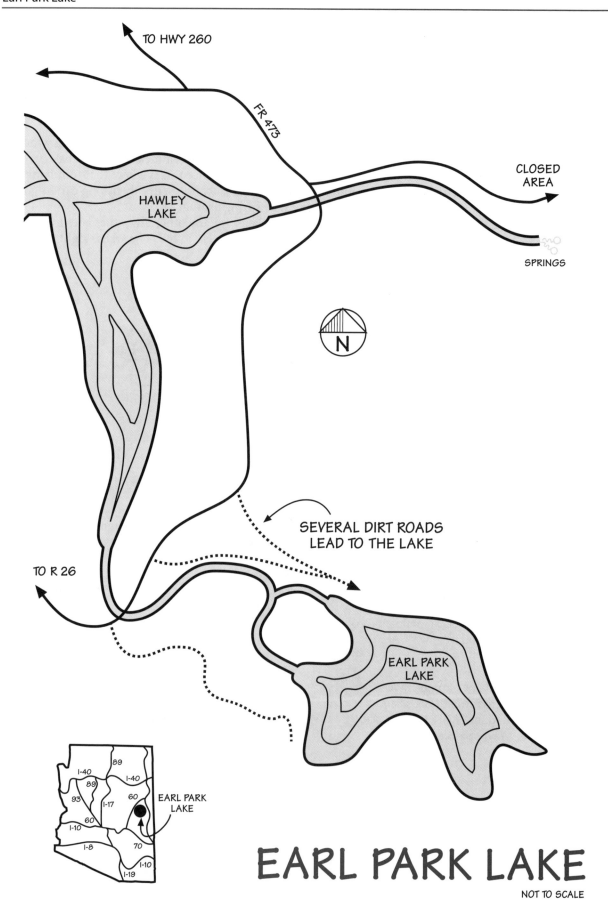

TO HWY 260

FR 473

CLOSED
AREA

HAWLEY
LAKE

SPRINGS

N

SEVERAL DIRT ROADS
LEAD TO THE LAKE

TO R 26

EARL PARK
LAKE

I-40   89
I-40
89   60
93   I-17   EARL PARK
60   LAKE
I-10
I-8   70
I-10
I-19

EARL PARK LAKE

NOT TO SCALE

Earl Park Lake

This small 42-acre lake is perfect for fishing from kick boat or float tube or by wading. Add its catch and release regulation to the scenic setting in the White Mountains, and Earl Park Lake is a "must-try" spot. Most of the weekend campers stop and fish nearby Hawley Lake, leaving Earl Park to the fly fishing crowd. The Apache, rainbow and brown trout here are good-sized and eager for the fly, at least for part of the day.

There is ample room on most of the shore for wading. Casts are protected from the wind by large trees and the canyon. The best way to fish this lake, however, is to use a fin-propelled boat. This provides access to the weed banks and drop-offs. Most fly fishers match the prolific, summer-long damselfly hatch. In late summer look for callibaetis and grasshoppers.

To get to Earl Park Lake from the Phoenix area, take any major Hwy. east to Pinetop. Take Hwy. 260 from Pinetop to the Hawley Lake turnoff, State Rte. 473. Proceed to Hawley Lake and follow the signs to Earl Park.

BURK'S ADULT
DAMSEL

SCHROEDER'S
PARA-HOPPER

Types of Fish
Apache, rainbow and brown trout.

Known Hatches
Lots of damselflies and grasshoppers in summer. Some callibaetis mayflies in the evening.

Equipment to Use
Rods: 6 weight, 9'.
Reels: Mechanical or disc drag is fine.
Line: Sinking and sink tips are best.
Leaders: 3X to 6X, 9' for floating line. 4X, 3' to 4' for sinking lines.
Wading: Wading and boating work well. Use a kick boat or float tube for best coverage.

Flies to Use
Dries: Adult Damselflies, #16–#18 Adams, Hoppers.
Nymphs: #16–#20 Damselfly, Gold-Ribbed Hare's Ears, Pheasant Tail.
Streamers: #8 brown, black, and olive Woolly Buggers.

When to Fish
Spring, summer, and fall.

Seasons & Limits
Freezes in the winter. Catch and release, artificial flies and lures only.

Accommodations & Services
Camping at Hawley Lake. Pinetop area has hotels, gas, groceries.

Nearby Fly Fishing
North Fork of the Black River.

Rating
Fish feed sporadically, so a good portion of the day is spent trying to figure them out. A solid 7.

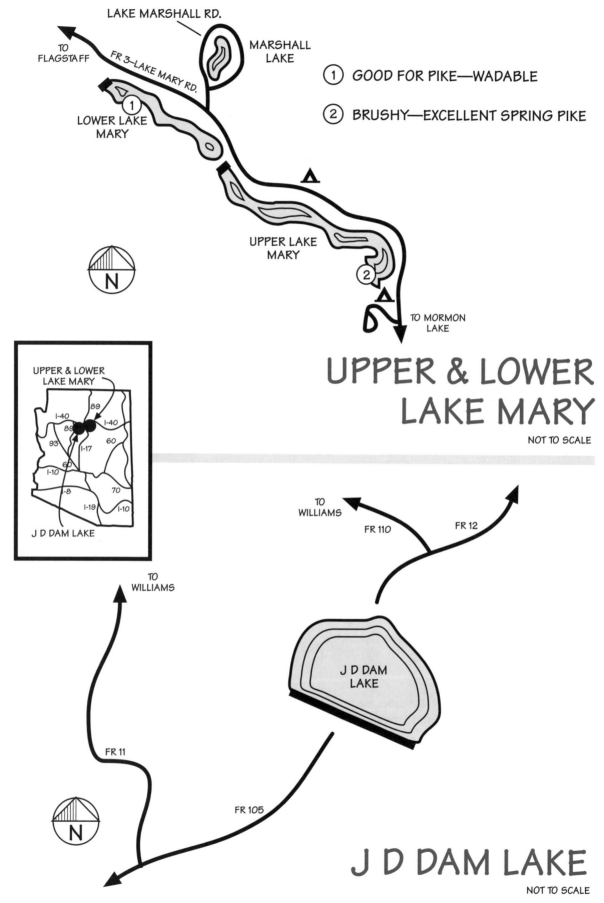

LAKE MARSHALL RD.

TO FLAGSTAFF

FR 3—LAKE MARY RD.

MARSHALL LAKE

① GOOD FOR PIKE—WADABLE

② BRUSHY—EXCELLENT SPRING PIKE

LOWER LAKE MARY

UPPER LAKE MARY

N

TO MORMON LAKE

UPPER & LOWER LAKE MARY

NOT TO SCALE

UPPER & LOWER LAKE MARY

I-40 89 I-40

89

93 I-17 60

60

I-10

I-8 70

I-19 I-10

J D DAM LAKE

TO WILLIAMS

FR 110 FR 12

TO WILLIAMS

J D DAM LAKE

N

FR 11

FR 105

J D DAM LAKE

NOT TO SCALE

Lake Mary & J D Dam

Over the years Upper and Lower Lake Mary and J D Dam have not been great places to fish. If that's where you happen to be, however, they can provide a day of fly fishing for trout and pike. Here's how they came to be.

The city of Flagstaff, at 7,000' elevation, is built on the remnants of a great volcanic field of porous rock. Most of the snow or rain goes underground so streams don't run down the mountain very well. Therefore, Flagstaff built Upper and Lower Lake Mary for water storage.

The two Lake Marys were built in a canyon just east of town in the Coconino National Forest. Upper Lake Mary is 600 acres. Both are lined with pines and cedars, have lots of picnic areas, and have small boat access.

J D Dam, another reservoir, is just south of Williams in the Kaibab National Forest. The 15 acres of lake is good kick boat water. It's been adopted by the fly fishing club in Flagstaff and can fish pretty well at times. Its leaky dam was recently renovated, and the lake level will probably be back to normal by the time you read this.

The best fly fishing approach on these lakes is to fish the weed beds and underwater structure from a kick boat. Floating lines work well during hatches. You can also fish grasshopper patterns. Sinking and sink tip lines are good for subsurface presentations.

Upper and Lower Lake Mary are on Lake Mary Road southeast of Flagstaff. To get to J D Dam take I-40 west from Flagstaff to the Williams exit. Go through Williams to FR 173 (Perkinsville Rd.), then take FR 110 east to FR 105. Turn right. The lake is right there.

Types of Fish
Rainbow and brown trout, bass, pike, sunfish.

Known Hatches & Baitfish
Damselflies, Baetis mayflies, crawfish, various minnows.

Equipment to Use
Rods: 6 weight, 9'.
Reels: Palm drag is fine.
Line: Floating, sinking, sink tip lines.
Leaders: 9' on floating lines; 3' on sinking lines. Wire tippets for pike.
Wading: Boating is best. Motors recommended on Upper Lake Mary.

Flies to Use
Dries: Adult Damselflies, #14–18 Adams.
Nymphs: Damselflies, #14–18 Hare's Ears, #16–18 Pheasant Tail.
Streamers/Poppers: Woolly Bugger, Peacock Lady, assorted poppers for the bass and pike.

When to Fish
Spring, summer, fall.

Seasons & Limits
Limits at Lake Mary and J D Dam seem to change often, so it is best to consult current Arizona fishing regulations. Generally artificial lures and flies only.

Accommodations & Services
Everything is available in Flagstaff and Williams.

Rating
Depending on weather, fish, and your luck, 4 to 6 .

1. CASTLE CREEK ARM
2. BOAT LAUNCH RAMPS
3. MAIN ENTRANCE—PAY STATION
4. SELF-PAY STATION
5. AREA CLOSED IN SPRING FOR BALD EAGLE NESTING
6. HUMBUG CREEK ARM
7. COLES BAY
8. GOOSE BAY

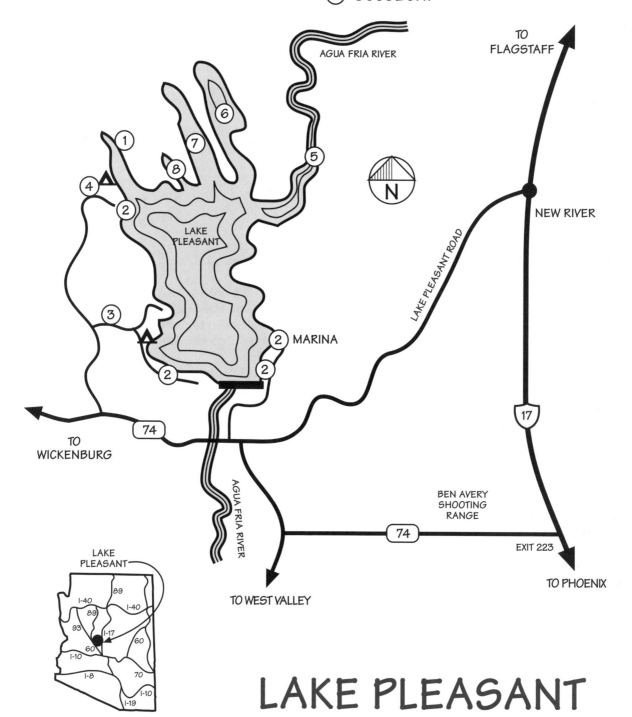

LAKE PLEASANT

NOT TO SCALE

Lake Pleasant

This desert lake offers lots of diverse structures that make it a great place to fly fish. Casting a popping bug against a saguaro cactus or over flooded ocotillo is quite an experience. This lake is a short drive from Phoenix and yields large bass in the double digits.

Arizona's best-known bass lake has been written up in bass fishing magazines for years. Almost 10,000 acres in size, it has tons of shoreline and many coves and arms worth exploring. The water in the lake fluctuates with the season and agricultural demand. It's generally clear, but if the lake begins to fill or drop rapidly it muddies up, which can affect fishing.

Top water Popping Bugs or Pencil Poppers, Hair Bugs, and Divers work well when the bass are feeding on shad. Also, fish the deeper water around submerged islands or off vertical walls with Clouser Minnows or weighted Woolly Buggers.

Anyone who fishes for bass knows that the hardest part is finding them. A high-powered motorboat is your best bet here. If you hate fly fishing from a bass boat, throw in a tube or kick boat to use once you've located bass. *Note:* Several reliable sources have told stories of being chased by rattlesnakes while in a tube or kick boat. It seems the rattlers think the boats are islands.

To get to Lake Pleasant from Phoenix, take I-17 north to the Carefree Hwy./ Lake Pleasant exit. Follow the signs west to the lake.

Types of Fish
Largemouth bass, smallmouth bass, white bass, crappie, and bluegills. Also carp, catfish, and some striped bass.

Known Hatches & Baitfish
Threadfin shad by the millions! Damselflies, dragonflies, mice, and rattlesnakes.

Equipment to Use
Rods: 8 or 9 weight, 9'.
Reels: Mechanical or disc drag is fine.
Line: Floating, sinking, sink tips.
Leaders: On sinking lines, 3' tapered to 12 lb.; on floating lines 6' to 9' tapered to 8 lb.
Wading: Bass boats, tubes, or kick boats. Chest-high waders and fins. Hip boots OK on the shore.

Flies to Use
Top water: Poppers, Divers, Wiggle Bugs, Hoppers, Damselflies, Dragonflies.
Subsurface: Water-Pups, Clouser Minnows, Water Snakes, Woolly Buggers.

When to Fish
Spring, mild fall days.

Seasons & Limits
Fish year-around. The limit for bass can change, so check current regulations.

Accommodations & Services
Near Phoenix. There is a private marina on the lake's east side. In the regional park there are two boat ramps, camping, and restrooms. This is a fee area.

Nearby Fly Fishing
Bartlett Reservoir.

Rating
Don't bother when the temperature moves the fish to deep water; an 8 most of the spring and fall.

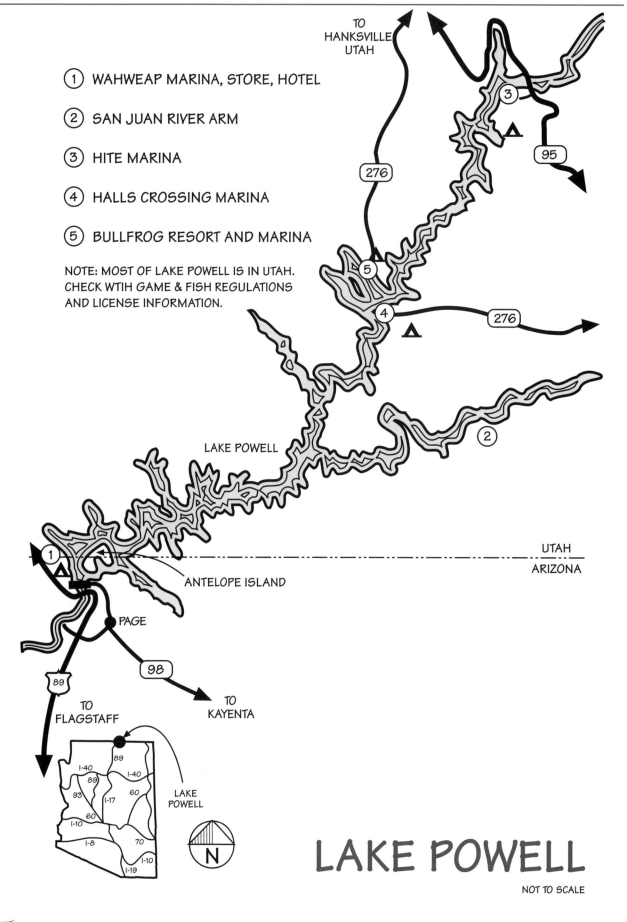

① WAHWEAP MARINA, STORE, HOTEL

② SAN JUAN RIVER ARM

③ HITE MARINA

④ HALLS CROSSING MARINA

⑤ BULLFROG RESORT AND MARINA

NOTE: MOST OF LAKE POWELL IS IN UTAH.
CHECK WTIH GAME & FISH REGULATIONS
AND LICENSE INFORMATION.

TO
HANKSVILLE
UTAH

276

95

LAKE POWELL

UTAH

ARIZONA

ANTELOPE ISLAND

PAGE

98

89

TO
FLAGSTAFF

TO
KAYENTA

I-40   89
I-40
89
93   60
I-17
60
I-10
70
I-8
I-10
I-19

LAKE
POWELL

N

LAKE POWELL

NOT TO SCALE

Lake Powell

Lake Powell draws thousands of families every year, who rent houseboats and disappear for a few days into the lake's many coves. These coves and shore structure are a draw for anglers, too. If the trip is timed right you can have good fly fishing for a number of warmwater species. A great way to experience the lake while fly fishing is to use a houseboat for a base and do your fishing from a bass boat.

The motorboat will allow you to cover enough water to find fish. The best approach is to find likely looking cover in coves and at drop-offs. Look for fish, especially striped bass, chasing shad.

This high desert lake is at 3,700' elevation. It was created by Glen Canyon Dam and is 800' deep in places. The 160,000 acres of water have 1,900 miles of shoreline that's lined with sand, rocks and desert vegetation within the breathtakingly beautiful Glen Canyon.

Lake Powell is accessed at the town of Page. To get to Page, go north on Hwy. 89 from Flagstaff.

LEFTY'S DECEIVER

Types of Fish
Largemouth bass, smallmouth bass, striped bass, crappie, carp, walleye, pike and sunfish.

Known Hatches & Baitfish
Lots of shad.

Equipment to Use
Rods: 8 weight, 9' for bass. 4 to 6 weight, 8-½ to 9' for panfish.
Reels: Disc or palm drag is fine.
Line: Floating, sinking, sink tip.
Leaders: Trout leaders to 12 lb. Regular bass leaders. Wire tippet for pike.
Boating: A good motorboat is recommended. A fast bass boat is best. Try using a houseboat as a base.

Flies to Use
Poppers, Clouser Minnows, Deceivers, Hoppers, small nymphs.

When to Fish
Spring is best, although it can be windy. Summer is second best and fall can be good.

Seasons & Limits
Unlimited bag limit on striped bass. Smallmouth have a limit of 20, and largemouth bass a limit of five. Check current regulations as limits can change.

Accommodations & Services
One of the largest marinas in the United States is Wahweap right outside Page, AZ. It offers food, lodging, and boat rentals.

Nearby Fly Fishing
Lees Ferry for big trout.

Rating
Because the lake's size makes finding fish difficult at times, a 6.

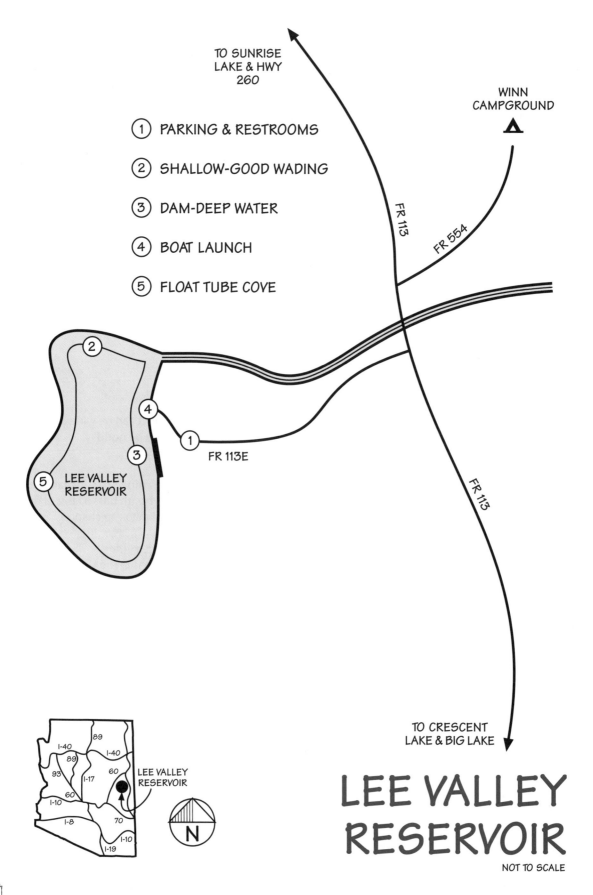

TO SUNRISE
LAKE & HWY
260

WINN
CAMPGROUND

1. PARKING & RESTROOMS
2. SHALLOW-GOOD WADING
3. DAM-DEEP WATER
4. BOAT LAUNCH
5. FLOAT TUBE COVE

FR 113

FR 554

1 FR 113E

2
4
3
5 LEE VALLEY
RESERVOIR

FR 113

TO CRESCENT
LAKE & BIG LAKE

LEE VALLEY
RESERVOIR

NOT TO SCALE

I-40
89
I-40
89
93
I-17
60
LEE VALLEY
RESERVOIR
60
I-10
I-8
70
I-10
I-19

N

Lee Valley Reservoir

Easy to get to and easy to get to know, Lee Valley is the perfect place to introduce a newcomer to the sport of fly fishing. It's also a good lake to stop by and fish for a couple of hours while touring the White Mountains. My young boys like to stop here and catch six or eight fish in a short time. We don't have to pump up a boat or put on a lot of gear.

Lee Valley Reservoir is on a forested plateau. It's small enough to walk around in a short time, and has many types of fly fishing water. Coves and points along with the weed banks that grow in midsummer are the best places to fish. The lake has good populations of Apache trout and grayling that like flies.

Both fish come into the shallows, so shore wading is a good way to cast for fish. Like most lakes, Lee Valley is best fished from a boat or tube, though. There are several good hatches of mayflies and caddis combined with grasshoppers and damselflies. This insect variety means many choices of flies and techniques. Most fly fishers go with a floating line and a dry fly approach. Sinking lines work well in midsummer.

To get to Lee Valley Reservoir, head to the White Mountains. From State Rte. 260, turn south on the Sunrise Lake road, Rte. 273. Continue on FR 113 when you enter the national forest. Drive past Sheeps Crossing on the Little Colorado until you see the sign for the lake on the right.

Types of Fish
Grayling and Apache trout.

Known Hatches
Damselflies, blue-winged olive, pale morning dun, callibaetis. Hoppers blow off the prairie on windy days.

Equipment to Use
Rods: 5 or 6 weight, 9'.
Reels: Mechanical or disc drag.
Line: Floating to full sink.
Leaders: 4X–6X, 9'.
Wading: Chest-high waders and boots or a float tube and fins, work equally well here. Take an anchor since it can be windy.

Flies to Use
Dries: Adams, BWOs, Hoppers, Blue Damselflies.
Nymphs: Pheasant Tail, Hare's Ear, Damselflies, Princes.
Streamers: Woolly Buggers.

When to Fish
Spring, summer, fall. The lake is frozen in the winter and the roads are impassable.

Seasons & Limits
Open all year, if fishable. Check regulations as limits change. Flies or artificial lures only.

Accommodations & Services
Store near Sunrise Lake and Greer; other services In Pinetop or 40 miles away in Springerville.

Nearby Fly Fishing
Sheeps Crossing on the Little Colorado River, West Fork of the Black River, Sunrise Lake, Crescent Lake.

Rating
A pleasant place for some easy fishing. The fish are small but readily take flies and the lake is generally beautiful. This lake dried up in 2003, but should refill in 2004 and will again be full of nice Apache trout and grayling.

① PARKING—MT. BALDY WILDERNESS

② BROOK TROUT

③ CANYON

④ SHEEPS CROSSING

⑤ X-DIAMOND RANCH

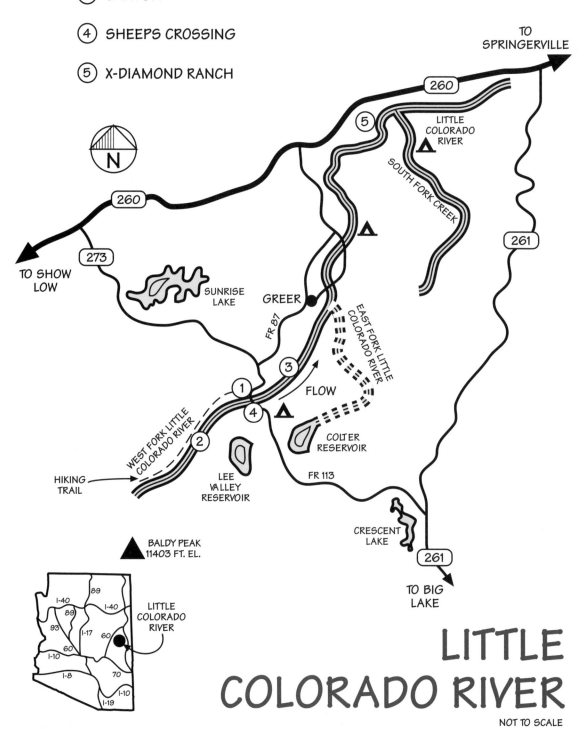

TO SPRINGERVILLE

260

5

LITTLE COLORADO RIVER

SOUTH FORK CREEK

261

260

273

TO SHOW LOW

SUNRISE LAKE

GREER

FR 87

EAST FORK LITTLE COLORADO RIVER

3

FLOW

1

4

COLTER RESERVOIR

WEST FORK LITTLE COLORADO RIVER

2

FR 113

HIKING TRAIL

LEE VALLEY RESERVOIR

CRESCENT LAKE

261

TO BIG LAKE

BALDY PEAK 11403 FT. EL.

I-40 89
I-40
89
93   I-17   60
60
I-10
I-8   70
I-10
I-19

LITTLE COLORADO RIVER

LITTLE COLORADO RIVER

NOT TO SCALE

Little Colorado River

One of the most pristine places in the state, this stream has cascading falls and plunge pools offering many opportunities to fish large dry flies or nymphs. The water is almost always crystal clear, except below the Greer Lakes. It even flows well enough in drought years to sustain fish populations. This is a very nice place to hike, and the fishing almost becomes secondary.

Originating from springs on Baldy Peak, the Little Colorado River ends at the Grand Canyon. The White Mountains headwaters hold brook, brown, rainbow, and the native Apache trout. Many serious fly fishers pass by this area because of the large number of bait fishers, kids, and dogs near most road pullouts. Don't let the crowds put you off, since average Arizonans won't usually wander more than 10' from their vehicle. Simply walk away from the road and you'll be in great wilderness.

At its headwaters, the Little Colorado is a small, clear creek lined with firs, pines, and willows. A dusty dirt road leading to and beyond the crossing is paved about a half mile on either side of Sheeps Crossing. This paving helps keep silt out of the stream. Between Sheeps Crossing and Greer, the stream flows through a tight, overgrown canyon. Downstream from Greer is the X-Diamond Ranch, a private fishery.

The best way to fish this area is with Hoppers, Stonefly imitations, or Caddis on the top. Usually the fish farther away from the road are not too picky. When the dries don't work, tie on a Pheasant Tail nymph or Hare's Ear. The favorite rig in these small streams is to tie a Dropper nymph off a large dry, such as a Hopper or Stimulator.

To get to the Little Colorado from Hwy. 260 take the Sunrise Lake turnoff, Indian Rd. 273, to FR 113. Continue to the bridge. At Greer take the Greer turnoff from 260. To get to the X-Diamond Ranch travel farther east on 260 and look for the South Fork sign about five miles from the Greer turnoff.

Types of Fish
Rainbow, brook, and brown trout.

Known Hatches
One of the most insect-prolific streams in Arizona. Caddis (tan and brown #4–18) stoneflies, (golden and brown #4–14), and Baetis mayflies. Annelids and leeches are present, so try San Juan Worms and Woolly Buggers when nothing else works.

Equipment to Use
Rods: 3 or 4 weight, 7-½'.
Reels: Mechanical or disc drag.
Line: Double taper, floating works best.
Leaders: 5X, 6'–8'.
Wading: Hip boots OK, as are waders and boots.

Flies to Use
Dries: Elk Hair Caddis, Stimulators, Hoppers, Ants, Adams, Blue-Winged Olives.
Nymphs: Hare's Ears, Pheasant Tails, Caddis larvae, and their Beadhead counterparts.
Streamers: Woolly Buggers.

When to Fish
Early spring is very good if the water isn't too high. Runoff is usually short-lived. Summer is good, but can be crowded. Fall can be *very* good.

Seasons & Limits
Fish all year; check regualtions for limits. I recommend releasing all or most brown trout, since they are not stocked. The private X-Diamond Ranch is catch and release.

Accommodations & Services
Lodging and stores near Sunrise Lake and Greer. Phone X-Diamond Ranch (928) 333-2286 for reservations.

Nearby Fly Fishing
Sunrise Lake, Lee Valley Lake, Black River and tributaries.

Rating
Easily an 8. The largest stream-dwelling fish in Arizona live in the X-Diamond stretch, which, though not easy, rates a 9.

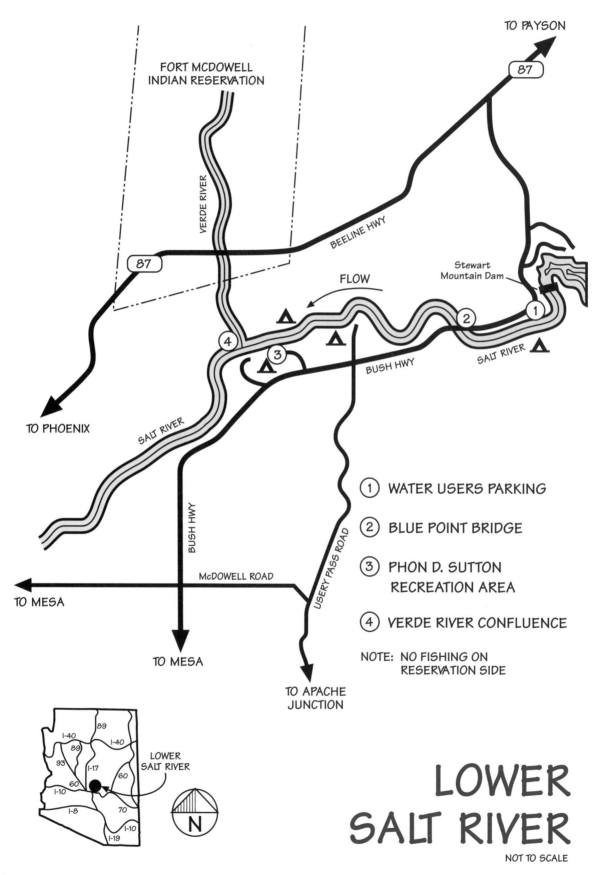

FORT MCDOWELL
INDIAN RESERVATION

TO PAYSON

87

VERDE RIVER

87

BEELINE HWY

Stewart
Mountain Dam

FLOW

2

1

4

3

SALT RIVER

BUSH HWY

TO PHOENIX

SALT RIVER

BUSH HWY

McDOWELL ROAD

TO MESA

TO MESA

USERY PASS ROAD

TO APACHE
JUNCTION

1 WATER USERS PARKING

2 BLUE POINT BRIDGE

3 PHON D. SUTTON
  RECREATION AREA

4 VERDE RIVER CONFLUENCE

NOTE: NO FISHING ON
RESERVATION SIDE

I-40   89
I-40
89
93   I-17
60   60
I-10
I-8   70
        I-10
     I-19

LOWER
SALT RIVER

N

LOWER
SALT RIVER

NOT TO SCALE

Lower Salt River

Only 40 minutes from downtown, the Salt River is metro Phoenix's closest fishery. It's very popular with fly fishers who don't have the time to travel to the high-elevation trout waters.

It's hard to believe such a beautiful canyon and creek are so close to a major city. Canyon walls several hundred feet high offer solitude for several types of birds, including at least one nesting pair of bald eagles. Coyotes and Javelina abound, as well do more than a few rattlesnakes.

Because the lower Salt originates deep below the surface of Saguaro Lake, its waters run cold and clear for most of the year. It's stocked with rainbow trout and there are bluegill, largemouth and smallmouth bass, and way too many suckers.

Anything will catch fish here, but nymphs and streamers produce the best results. There are some caddis and mayflies, but the hatches generally are not strong enough to interest the fish.

The only drawbacks to fishing the lower Salt are all the garbage left by bait fishers, the day users, and the multitudes of recreational tubers that flock to the river in hot weather. Since this is primarily an irrigation and flood control channel, water flows are sometimes turned down to a trickle.

To get to the lower Salt from Scottsdale proceed through Fountain Hills on Shea Blvd. to Hwy. 87 (Beeline Hwy). Take the Saguaro Lake and Salt River Recreation area exit. From the East Valley take the Beeline Hwy. directly from Apache Junction.

Types of Fish
Suckers, bass, bluegill, stocked rainbow trout.

Known Hatches
Some green caddis, Baetis and pale evening dun mayflies and lots of midges. Large hatch of inner tubes in the summer months.

Equipment to Use
Rods: 5 weight, 9'.
Reels: Palm or disc drag is fine.
Line: Floating.
Leaders: 4X–5X, 7-½' to 9'.
Wading: All types of wading gear are used here, including sneakers.

Flies to Use
Dries: #14–16 Blue Winged Olive, #12–20 Adams, Elk Hair Caddis, attractors, Hoppers.
Nymphs: PT's, Caddis larvae, Hare's Ears.
Streamers: Woolly Buggers.

When to Fish
Whenever you can, providing there is enough water. In the late fall or early winter the water flow can be as low as 8 cfs from the dam to the Sutton Recreation Area. This is where the Verde enters to raise water high enough to fish. Go early during the summer to avoid the swimmers.

Seasons & Limits
Year-round. Limits can vary, so check state regulations.

Accommodations & Services
Everything is available in Phoenix and surrounding towns.

Nearby Fly Fishing
Saguaro Lake and other waters on the way to the White Mountains.

Rating
Stocked trout, suckers in the way, uninspired hatches and fly fishing next to bait fishers, garbage and ATVs is not pleasing to most fly fishers. Nearby, but only a 4.

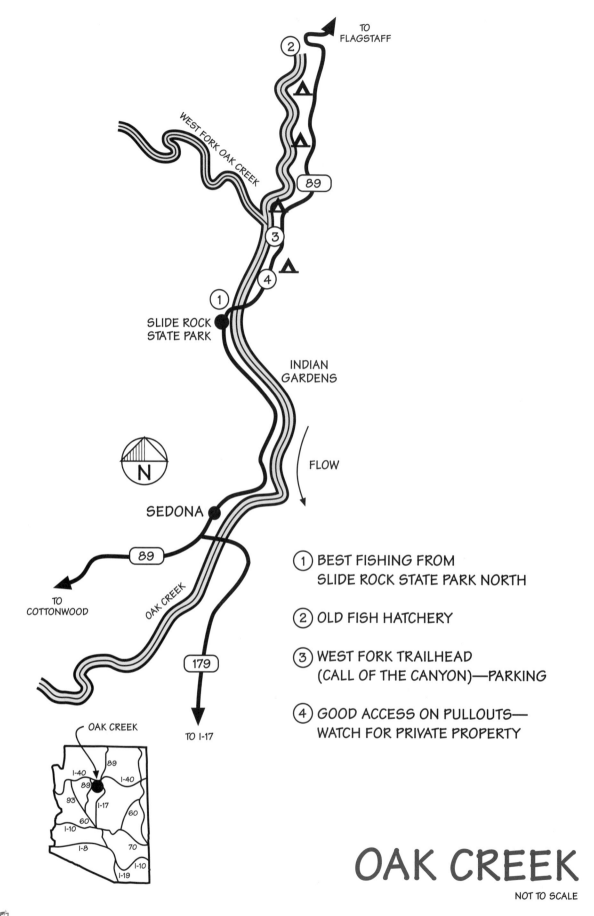

TO
FLAGSTAFF

②

89

WEST FORK OAK CREEK

③

④

①

SLIDE ROCK
STATE PARK

INDIAN
GARDENS

N

FLOW

SEDONA

89

TO
COTTONWOOD

OAK CREEK

179

TO I-17

① BEST FISHING FROM
SLIDE ROCK STATE PARK NORTH

② OLD FISH HATCHERY

③ WEST FORK TRAILHEAD
(CALL OF THE CANYON)—PARKING

④ GOOD ACCESS ON PULLOUTS—
WATCH FOR PRIVATE PROPERTY

OAK CREEK

OAK CREEK

NOT TO SCALE

I-40   89
I-40   I-40
89
93
I-17
60
60
I-10
I-8   70
I-10
I-19

Oak Creek

Anyone who has ever visited Arizona has been to or heard of the beautiful red rock country of Sedona. Few of these visitors realize that the small creek running through town is one of the finest trout streams in the Southwest. Oak Creek is spring-fed from the upper reaches of Oak Creek Canyon. It flows 42 miles to the Verde River, and the upper canyon section holds good trout. Beyond the Page Springs area the water becomes too warm for trout.

The creek flows cold and clear and fishes well most of the year. The exceptions are during the brief spring runoff period or the occasional gully washer. The gradient is high near the top of the canyon but mellows around the confluence of the West Fork of Oak Creek. From here downstream there are lots of riffles and pools that test a fly fisher's skills. Some parts of the creek canyon are tight and require a short rod and casting prowess, while other sections are wide open with more than enough room for even a 9' rod.

The canyon is awe-inspiring when the Navajo sandstone is lit brilliant red by the high desert sun. There are plenty of pullouts for fishing access along the road, although a short hike or climb into the canyon is sometimes necessary to get away from the picnic crowd. This fishery has suffered from overstocking by the Game & Fish Department, as have most of the fisheries in Arizona.

The best way to fish here is with a large attractor dry fly or Hopper on top. Tie a Hare's Ear or Pheasant Tail nymph about 20" below. Most anglers use Beadheads.

When an authentic hatch occurs—usually afternoon Baetis—use a #20 Adams Parachute. Woolly Buggers in the deep pools and under banks sometimes lure large brown trout. Browns here are wild and can usually be found away from the road and camping areas. Oak Creek has a healthy population of these great fish, but many anglers simply are not skilled enough to catch them.

To reach Oak Creek from Phoenix take I-17 north to State Route 179. From Sedona continue north.

Types of Fish
Rainbow trout, wild brown trout.

Known Hatches
Baetis (BWO), Heptogenia (PED), little brown stonefly, a few tricos.

Equipment to Use
Rods: 3 or 4 weight, 7-½'.
Reels: Palm drag is fine.
Line: Floating, double taper.
Leaders: 6X, 7-½' to 9'.
Wading: Lightweight waders and boots are fine, as are hip boots. Wading is very easy, but some hiking is in order.

Flies to Use
Dries: #12–20 Parachute Adams or Hoppers in summer and fall; #8–12 Madam X or Stimulator in spring and early summer.
Nymphs: Pheasant Tails, Hare's Ears, Little Brown Stoneflies.
Streamers: Woolly Bugger.

When to Fish
Anytime, but the summer months are extremely crowded with sightseers and college kids from NAU in Flagstaff.

Seasons & Limits
Fish all year. Limits change so check Arizona regulations. I highly recommend catch and release for brown trout. The west fork of Oak Creek and the creek from Junipine resort to the west fork are catch and release with single barbless hooks.

Accommodations & Services
All services are available in Sedona and Flagstaff.

Nearby Fly Fishing
Lake Mary near Flagstaff.

Rating
The rating would be higher if the stream weren't such a tourist spot and weren't stocked, nonetheless, an 8.

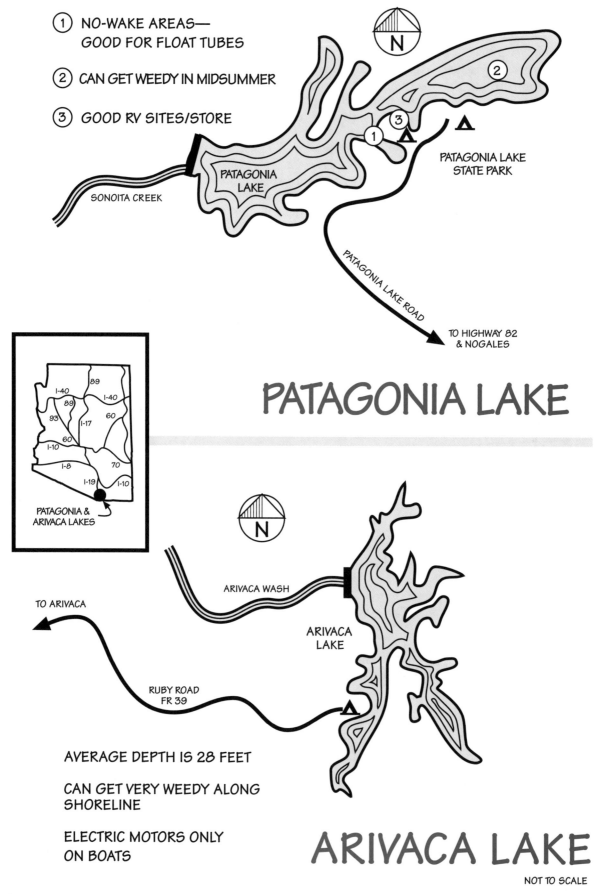

① NO-WAKE AREAS—
GOOD FOR FLOAT TUBES

② CAN GET WEEDY IN MIDSUMMER

③ GOOD RV SITES/STORE

N

②

③ ①

PATAGONIA LAKE
STATE PARK

PATAGONIA
LAKE

SONOITA CREEK

PATAGONIA LAKE ROAD

TO HIGHWAY 82
& NOGALES

PATAGONIA LAKE

I-40 89
I-40
93 89 60
I-17
60
I-10
I-8 70
I-19 I-10

PATAGONIA &
ARIVACA LAKES

N

ARIVACA WASH

TO ARIVACA

ARIVACA
LAKE

RUBY ROAD
FR 39

AVERAGE DEPTH IS 28 FEET

CAN GET VERY WEEDY ALONG
SHORELINE

ELECTRIC MOTORS ONLY
ON BOATS

ARIVACA LAKE

NOT TO SCALE

Patagonia & Arivaca Lakes

For southern Arizona bass, bluegill, and crappie fishing, these small lakes not far from Tucson are ideal for fly rodders. Patagonia Lake is 265 acres in size and makes a great little fishing escape. It tends to be crowded in the summer. Arivaca Lake is small and its water level fluctuates a lot, but it has a reputation for better than average fishing. It has red-ear sunfish up to two pounds. Try that on your 4 weight!

Both lakes can be waded with great success, but a kick boat or float tube are the best way to go. Use standard bass-fishing techniques.

To get to Patagonia Lake, take I-10 east from Tucson to exit 281, exiting south on Hwy. 83 to Sonoita, then turn west on Hwy. 82 to the turnoff. To get to Arivaca Lake, take I-19 south from Tucson to exit 48 at Arivaca Junction. Then take Hwy. 22 (Arivaca Road) west to the town of Arivaca. Go south on 216 to FR39 (Ruby Road). Take 39 to the lake.

LEFTY'S DECEIVER

PENCIL POPPER

Types of Fish
Largemouth bass, bluegill, sunfish, crappie, and trout (in the winter).

Known Baitfish
Shad, minnows.

Equipment to Use
Rods: 4 to 8 weight, 8-½ to 9'.
Line: Floating, sinking, or sink tip.
Leaders: Trout and bass leaders in the 10 lb. range.
Wading: Kick boats or float tubes are best, but lightweight waders also work.

Flies to Use
Dries: Hoppers, Adams for the sunfish.
Nymphs: Hare's Ears, Pheasant Tails.
Streamers/Poppers: Poppers, Deceivers, Clouser Minnows, Woolly Buggers.

When to Fish
Spring, summer, and fall for bass; winter for bass and trout.

Seasons & Limits
Arivaca is catch and release for Bass. Check current regulations for limits.

Accommodations & Services
Patagonia Lake has a store with gas and camping. Arivaca Lake is near the town of Arivaca.

Nearby Fly Fishing
Nothing nearby.

Rating
Pretty much all that's around, a 5.

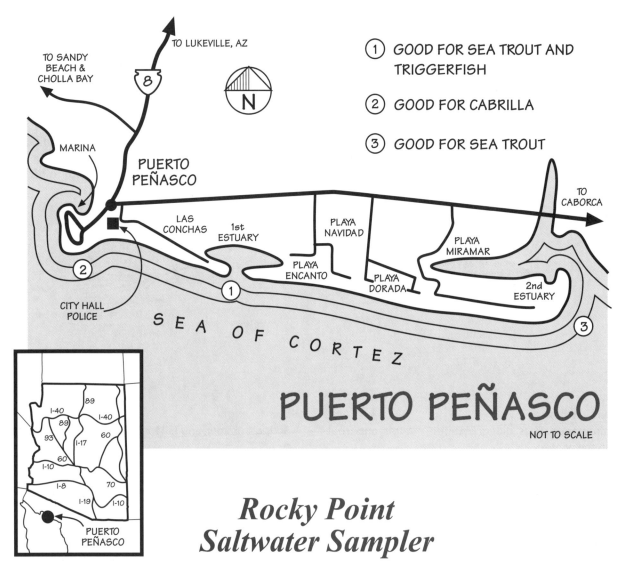

① GOOD FOR SEA TROUT AND TRIGGERFISH

② GOOD FOR CABRILLA

③ GOOD FOR SEA TROUT

TO SANDY BEACH & CHOLLA BAY

TO LUKEVILLE, AZ

8

N

MARINA

PUERTO PEÑASCO

LAS CONCHAS

1st ESTUARY

PLAYA NAVIDAD

TO CABORCA

PLAYA ENCANTO

PLAYA MIRAMAR

PLAYA DORADA

2nd ESTUARY

CITY HALL POLICE

②

①

③

S E A   O F   C O R T E Z

PUERTO PEÑASCO

NOT TO SCALE

I-40
89
I-40
89
93
60
I-17
60
I-10
I-8
70
I-19
I-10

PUERTO PEÑASCO

Rocky Point Saltwater Sampler

A few of the species fly fishers might hook at Puerto Peñasco

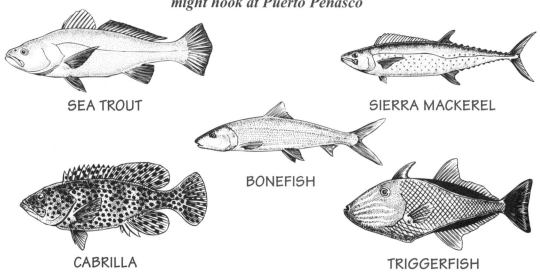

SEA TROUT

SIERRA MACKEREL

BONEFISH

CABRILLA

TRIGGERFISH

Puerto Peñasco, Mexico
Rocky Point

Imagine driving along a sandy beach looking for baitfish busting the surface. Then, one or two quick casts and, bingo, you're on to a fight better than any trout can put up. Later, with a cerveza frîa (cold beer), you can relate your stories of landing sea trout and pompano. From the Phoenix area, a 4-½ hour drive, about an hour of which is south of the border, will get you into fly fishing in the Sea of Cortez.

Expect warm blue-green seawater, inviting beaches, sand dunes, and enough fish ranging from two to ten lbs. to keep most of us happy. Fishing ranges from incredible to so-so. It can be windy during spring and winter. In early summer and fall, when temperatures are 65–70°, conditions are ideal.

You can drive to all major fishing spots, including the two estuaries east of town, Sandy Beach west of town, and Cholla Bay farther west. A boat (car topper or larger) covers the most water. The run to the second estuary is about 15 minutes by boat, 26 miles by car.

Rocky Point is a great place to learn the tricks of saltwater fly fishing. This streamer fishing involves heavy rods (7 to 9 weight), heavy flies and a short strong tippet. The best overall line is intermediate sink. Use floating lines only in very shallow areas. Look for schooling fish, cast a streamer in their path, and strip the line back very fast. Then, *hang on*!

If you don't find schooling fish, cast a weighted fly near rocky or marly (pebbly or stoney), areas and let it sink to the bottom. Usually within 6 to 10 slow, deliberate strips, cabrilla (rock bass) or triggerfish strike. Don't let the fish take much line. They'll hide in the rocks and you'll be lucky to get the fly back. If fish bite off more than two flies go up to 50 pound mono or wire tippet.

To reach Rocky Point from Phoenix take I-10 to Hwy. 85 south. Go through Gila Bend and Ajo to Lukeville, where you enter Mexico at Sonoita. Take Mex 8 south to Puerto Peñasco. Get Mexican auto insurance from your agent or in Ajo. It costs $30–$40 for two or three days. Carry your passport or original birth certificate and driver's license at all times.

Types of Fish
Corvina, (sea trout), pompano (leatherback jack), sierra, cabrilla (rock bass), and triggerfish. There may be others, as you never know what you might catch in saltwater. I have caught several bonefish and flounder.

Known Baitfish
Baitfish here are 2"–4".

Equipment to Use
Rods: 7 to 9 weight, 9'.
Reels: Saltwater anodized with a smooth disc drag. Don't scrimp.
Line: Intermediate, floating, sinking.
Leaders: Bonefish or saltwater tapered to 10–20 lbs. Fish are not leader shy. Wire leaders to 30 lb.
Wading: Wet wade with booties or sandals. A motorboat is the way to go.

Flies to Use
#8–1/0 Chartreuse and white or all-white Clouser Minnow. Poppers, all sizes and colors work. #4–1/0 White Deceiver. #6–2 Green/white and blue/white Bendback.

When to Fish
May to November is best. October is very good for sea trout. Fish the shore during low light, early morning and late afternoon. Sight cast midday. Inshore fishes best morning and evening.

Accommodations & Services
There is camping on the beach, if you can get there. Several clean, yet rustic hotels are in town. Try the Vina del Mar at the end of the road near the fish market. All restaurants have good food. Ask around.

The boat launch in the marina charges a small fee, but they watch your rig during the day.

Rating
On a good day, a 9. On a poor windy day, a 2. That's saltwater fishing! There's always a cerveza frîa waiting.

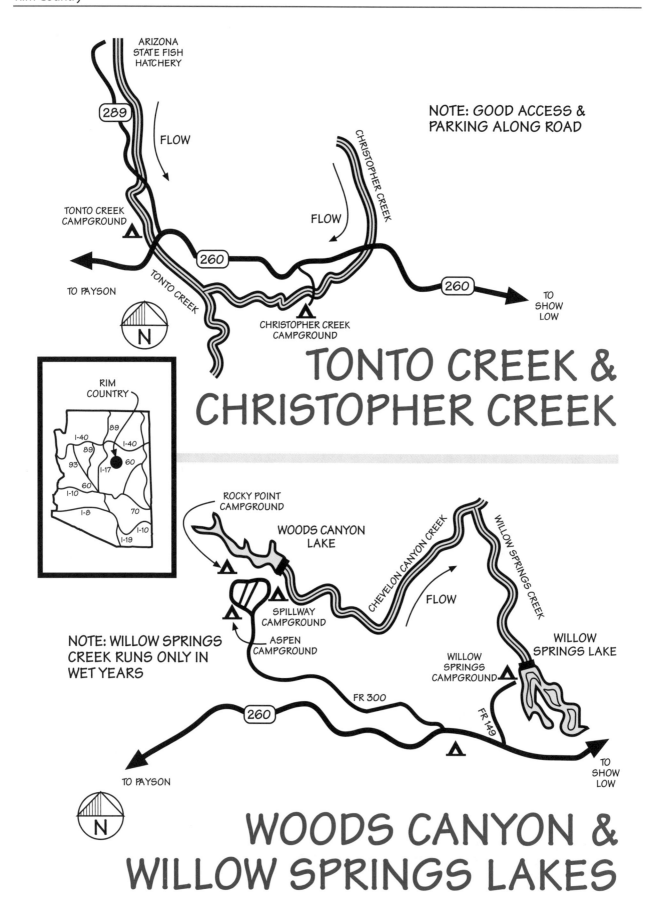

ARIZONA STATE FISH HATCHERY

289

FLOW

NOTE: GOOD ACCESS & PARKING ALONG ROAD

CHRISTOPHER CREEK

FLOW

TONTO CREEK CAMPGROUND

260

TO PAYSON

TONTO CREEK

N

CHRISTOPHER CREEK CAMPGROUND

260

TO SHOW LOW

TONTO CREEK & CHRISTOPHER CREEK

RIM COUNTRY

89
I-40   I-40
89   60
93   I-17
60
I-10
I-8   70
I-10
I-19

ROCKY POINT CAMPGROUND

WOODS CANYON LAKE

CHEVELON CANYON CREEK

WILLOW SPRINGS CREEK

FLOW

SPILLWAY CAMPGROUND

ASPEN CAMPGROUND

WILLOW SPRINGS LAKE

NOTE: WILLOW SPRINGS CREEK RUNS ONLY IN WET YEARS

WILLOW SPRINGS CAMPGROUND

FR 300

260

FR 149

TO PAYSON

TO SHOW LOW

N

WOODS CANYON & WILLOW SPRINGS LAKES

NOT TO SCALE

Rim Country

Tonto & Chistopher Creeks, Woods Canyon & Willow Springs Lakes

Here's a great area to fly fish when time is a factor. The Rim Country is the closest real fly fishing to Phoenix and provides urbanites a pleasant one-day outing. The elevation here doesn't get much over 6,000' so there are lots of piñon and ponderosa pines here. The lakes offer good trout fishing almost any time, while the stream fishing depends on the water flows.

The streams are spring fed with occasional runoff water that helps increase flows. The streams, however, can get extremely low. In the past 10 years new developments in the area have reduced the water level. Christopher Creek has been practically de-watered for most of the year. Both creeks, as well as the lakes, are put-and-take, with only a few holdover rainbows or some wild brown trout available.

The streams are easy to wade, but you have to be sneaky. It's best to fish the lakes from a kick boat or float tube.

To get to this area from Phoenix, take Hwy. 87 north and east to Payson. From Flagstaff take I-40 east to Hwy. 99 south. From Payson take Hwy. 260 east to the turnoffs for each lake. Follow the signs. Hwy. 260 crosses both streams.

Types of Fish
Rainbow and brown trout.

Known Hatches
Baetis mayflies, caddis, stoneflies. damselflies in the lakes.

Equipment to Use
Rods: Creeks, 3 or 4 weight, 7-½'; Lakes, 5 weight, 9'; streams, 6 weight, 9'.
Line: Floating, sinking, sink tip.
Leaders: 6X, 7-½' to 9' on floating lines. 4X, 3' on sinking lines.
Wading: Hip boots or lightweight waders for the creeks and streams. A float tube is best for the lakes.

Flies to Use
Dries: #16–20 Adams, #8–14 Damsel adults, Stimulator, #12–16 Caddis, Hopper, large attractors.
Nymphs: #16 Caddis pupae, #16–20 Pheasant Tails, #14–16 Hare's Ears. Beaded or unbeaded #10 Damselfly nymphs for the lakes.
Streamers: Woolly Buggers in the lakes.

When to Fish
Spring, summer, and fall. Winter depending on the weather.

Seasons & Limits
Statewide limits can change, see Arizona regulations.

Accommodations & Services
Everything available at Payson, Kohl's Ranch, or Christopher Creek.

Nearby Fly Fishing
Canyon Creek.

Rating
For fly fishing near town, a 6. A 4 if the water is too low.

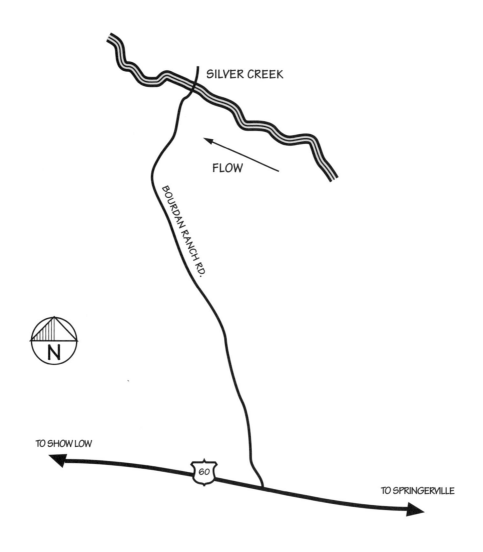

SILVER CREEK

FLOW

BOURDAN RANCH RD.

N

TO SHOW LOW

60

TO SPRINGERVILLE

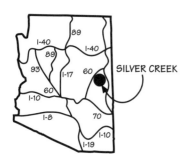

I-40
89
I-40
89
93
I-17
60
SILVER CREEK
60
I-10
I-8
70
I-10
I-19

SILVER CREEK

NOT TO SCALE

Silver Creek

This is the only public stream in Arizona where you can land a monster over 25 inches! This stream is stocked several times a year with nice catchable rainbow and Apache trout and occasionally with brood stock from the nearby hatchery.

Silver Creek is a true spring creek. Because of its elevation it tends to be extremely silty, making wading almost impossible. The banks are stable, however, and staying out of the water is seldom a problem. There are approximately two miles of riffles, pools, pocket water, and undercut banks.

Because the regulations are set up as a split season, the winter is the best time for a fly fisher to catch the big guys. The winter season is catch and release with single barbless hooks. The summer season runs from April 1 to September 30 and allows for bait fishing as well as harvesting.

Located just 3-½ hours from Phoenix, Silver Creek is 12 miles north of Show Low. From Show Low take Hwy. 60 toward Springerville. Turn left on Bourden Ranch Road and drive about 3.5 miles to the Silver Creek Hatchery turnoff.

Types of Fish
Apache and rainbow trout.

Known Hatches
Caddis and some Baetis mayflies, pale morning duns, golden and yellow sally stoneflies, and lots of grasshoppers and ants in the summer. Midges in the winter.

Equipment to Use
Rods: A 4 or 5 weight, 7-½' to 9' long.
Line: Standard double taper or weight forward floating.
Leaders: 4X or 5X, 7-½' or 9'.
Wading: Hippers are OK, but I always wear chest waders in the winter.

Flies to Use
For the winter season use midges, nymphs such as Pheasant Tails and Hare's Ears and Buggers.

When to Fish
Best in winter.

Seasons & Limits
From October 1 to April 1, catch and release with single barbless hooks. From April 1 to September 30, bait and barbed hooks are allowed and the angler may keep six trout. Always check current regulations as they may change.

Accommodations & Services
Everything is available in nearby Show Low and Springerville.

Nearby Fly Fishing
The X-Diamond Ranch (private), the White River and its north Fork, and lots of lakes.

Rating
A fun place to fish, although the idea of catching spawned-out brood stock doesn't appeal to a lot of folks. Also the silty conditions take away a bit of the beauty. I'll rate it a 7 in the winter and a solid 5 in the summer.

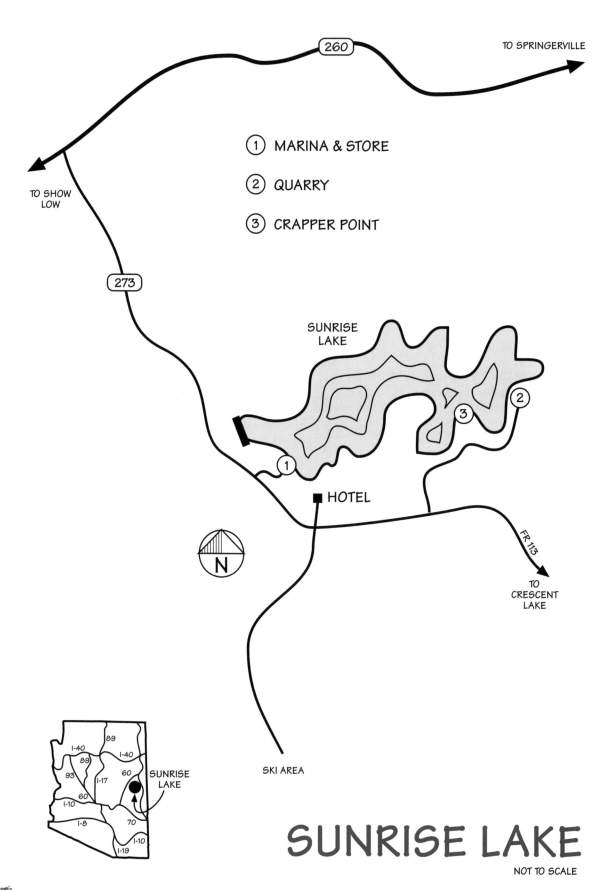

260

TO SPRINGERVILLE

1 MARINA & STORE

2 QUARRY

3 CRAPPER POINT

TO SHOW
LOW

273

SUNRISE
LAKE

1

3

2

HOTEL

N

FR 113

TO
CRESCENT
LAKE

SKI AREA

I-40   89
I-40
89
93   I-17   60   SUNRISE
60   LAKE
I-10
I-8   70
I-10
I-19

SUNRISE LAKE

NOT TO SCALE

Sunrise Lake

The jewel of the White Mountain Apache Reservation, Sunrise is the lake to fly fish for large trout or when you need a pleasant day of float fishing. The lake is easy to get to, easy to put a boat in, and easy to fish. The trout are larger here than on many other waters, so Sunrise is the favorite of most Arizona lake fishers!

Sunrise is fairly large at slightly more than 800 acres, depending on runoff. At the cool elevation of 9,100', it sits at the base of Mounts Ord and Baldy, home of the Sunrise Ski Area. Mountain snowpack feeds the majority of the area's streams and lakes. The lake can be windy in the spring, but by summer it is generally very agreeable.

In the late 1990s, Sunrise had some severe fish kills due to extremely thick ice caused by colder than normal winters. The lake usually bounces back quickly, though, and as of this writing Sunrise is fishing well.

Sunrise is a float tube and kick boat heaven. Fish this lake like any other by looking for submerged weed banks or structure where you can cast Woolly Buggers or streamers. When there's a hatch, fish it. It will probably be a callibaetis mayfly hatch, which occurs on most Arizona mountain lakes throughout the summer. The best action comes, however, when the damselflies hatch, and hatch they do!

Sunrise Lake is about 160 miles north and east of Phoenix, or the same distance east and south of Flagstaff. To get to the lake take Hwy. 260 from Pinetop or Springerville and follow the signs.

Types of Fish
Rainbow, brook, and Apache trout. Some grayling.

Known Hatches & Baitfish
Callibaetis and Baetis mayflies, damselflies. Lots of minnows. Some leeches and scuds.

Equipment to Use
Rods: 6 weight, 9'.
Reels: Palm drag will do.
Line: Floating, sinking, sink tip.
Leaders: 3X–6X, 9' for floating lines. 3X to 10 lb., 3' for sinking lines.
Wading: Kick boats or float tubes are best. Bring chest-high waders and fins.

Flies to Use
Dries: #14–18 Adams, Damselfly adults, Hopper, Ant.
Nymphs: Damselfly, #14 gray Scud, #14–18 Pheasant Tails, Hare's Ear.
Streamers: Woolly Buggers, Mickey Finns, Blacknosed Dace, Peacock Ladies.

When to Fish
Spring, summer, fall.

Seasons & Limits
Regulations change. See the White Mountain Apache National Forest regulations booklet.

Accommodations & Services
Hotel, store, and marina at the lake. Towns of Greer and Pinetop are close and have all other services.

Nearby Fly Fishing
Little Colorado River, Lee Valley Reservoir.

Rating
A 6 to an 8, depending on winter ice.

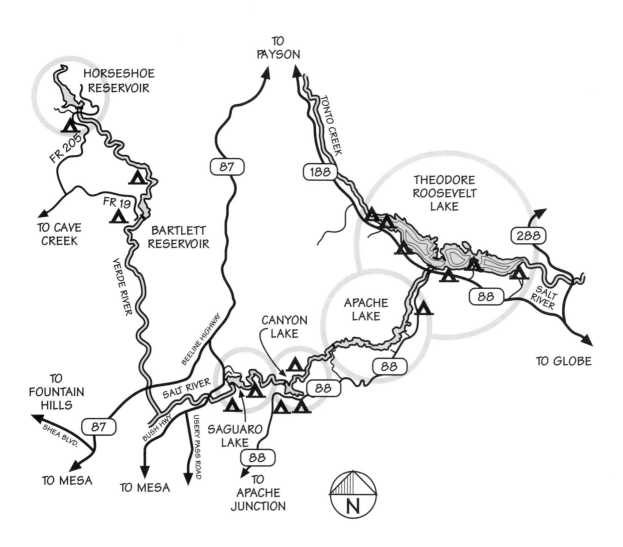

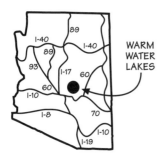

WARM WATER LAKES

NOT TO SCALE

Warm Water Lakes

Horseshoe Reservoir on the Verde River, Roosevelt, Apache, Canyon, & Saguaro Lakes on the Salt River

Winter locks Arizona's mountain trout streams in snow and ice, while spring floods fill them with winter runoff. If you're looking to wet a line during these seasons, our warmwater lakes are just the places for you. The bass fishing can be very good in the spring, as well as in the fall if the temperatures aren't too cold. All these lakes are close to Phoenix and make for an easy day trip.

Most fly fishers have fallen into a groove of fishing only for trout. This isn't necessarily practical in Arizona for much of the year. That's when bass, pike, bluegill, crappie, and even carp fishing can save what could be a terribly boring winter.

These lakes can be your ticket out of the winter doldrums. All these stillwaters were formed by dams on the Verde and Salt rivers. This water storage provides irrigation for farms in the Valley of the Sun and for Phoenix metro area's drinking water. They're surrounded by deep canyon walls and saguaro and ocotillo cactus. Quite a backdrop for fly fishing!

It's best to fish these waters from a motorboat so you can move around enough to find fish. Horseshoe Reservoir can become too low to launch a large bass boat. At these times, go with a kick boat or float tube.

Reach Horseshoe Reservoir by driving to Bartlett Reservoir on Cave Creek Road and Horseshoe Dam Road. Roosevelt is reached by taking the Roosevelt Lake turnoff (Hwy. 188) from Hwy. 87 or by taking the Apache Trail (Hwy. 88) from the East Valley. This route is also the best way to access Apache and Canyon lakes. Saguaro Lake is best reached from Hwy. 87.

Type of Fish
Bass, crappie, bluegill, pike, and carp.

Known Baitfish
Threadfin shad and various minnows.

Equipment to Use
Rods: 6 to 9 weight, 9'.
Reels: Palm or disc drag works fine.
Line: Floating, sinking, sink tip.
Leaders: Bass leaders from 6 to 9', tapered to 10 lbs.
Wading/Boating: Motorboats help to cover more water, but many coves can be fished using a kick boat or float tube. Bring chest-high waders and fins.

Flies to Use
Dries: Deer Hair bugs, grasshopper patterns.
Nymphs: Pheasant Tail, Prince.
Streamers/Poppers: Poppers, Clouser Minnows, shad patterns, Woolly Buggers.

When to Fish
Spring, winter, fall.

Seasons & Limits
Seasons and limits can change for all these waters. Please check current Arizona regulations.

Accommodations & Services
All services available in Phoenix and other nearby towns.

Rating
Depending on the time of year and species pursued, Apache and Canyon Lakes 6–8, the others 6.

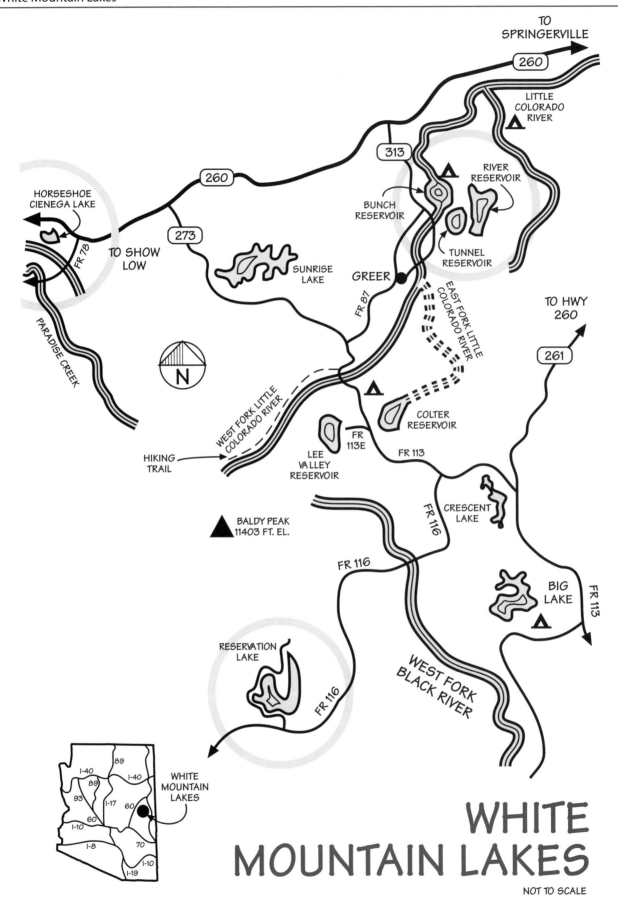

TO
SPRINGERVILLE

260

LITTLE
COLORADO
RIVER

313

RIVER
RESERVOIR

BUNCH
RESERVOIR

HORSESHOE
CIENEGA LAKE

260

TUNNEL
RESERVOIR

TO SHOW
LOW

273

SUNRISE
LAKE

GREER

FR 78

PARADISE CREEK

FR 87

EAST FORK LITTLE
COLORADO RIVER

TO HWY
260

261

N

WEST FORK LITTLE
COLORADO RIVER

COLTER
RESERVOIR

HIKING
TRAIL

FR 113E

FR 113

LEE
VALLEY
RESERVOIR

CRESCENT
LAKE

FR 116

BALDY PEAK
11403 FT. EL.

FR 116

BIG
LAKE

FR 113

RESERVATION
LAKE

FR 116

WEST FORK
BLACK RIVER

I-40

89

I-40

89

93

I-17

60

60

WHITE
MOUNTAIN
LAKES

I-10

70

I-8

I-10

I-19

WHITE
MOUNTAIN LAKES

NOT TO SCALE

White Mountain Lakes
Greer Area Reservoirs, Reservation Lake, Horseshoe Cienega Reservoirs/Lake, for a Change of Pace

When you tire of the more better-known White Mountain lakes, try these out for a change of scenery. These five lakes, as well as several others in the White Mountains, offer opportunities to get away from the most popular mountain lakes and still catch reasonable numbers of fish.

These lakes are all relatively small, easy to get to, and generally good fishing. The Greer Reservoirs tend to be muddy or off-color, due to seasonal drawdowns. Employ classic lake-flies and techniques like fishing Damsels and Woolly Buggers with floating, sinking, and sink-tip lines.

The Greer Reservoirs are off Hwy. 373 heading into Greer. Horseshoe Cienega Lake is right off Hwy. 260 between the Hawley Lake turnoff and the Sunrise Lake turnoff. Reservation is a little harder to find. Take the Sunrise Lake turnoff from Hwy. 260 and drive to Forest Road 116, then turn onto Y20.

ARIZONA
PEACOCK LADY

PARACHUTE ADAMS

DAVE'S HOPPER

Types of Fish
Apache, brown, rainbow, and brook trout.

Known Hatches
Damselflies, callibaetis, Baetis, grasshoppers.

Equipment to Use
Rods: 6 weight, 9'.
Reels: Palm drag is fine.
Line: Floating, sinking, and sink tip.
Leaders: 3' on sinking line, 9' on floating line.
Wading: Best fished from a kick boat or float tube.

Flies to Use
Dries: #14–18 Adams, adult Damsels, Hoppers.
Nymphs: Damsel, Pheasant Tail, Hare's Ear.
Streamers: Woolly Buggers, Peacock Ladies.

When to Fish
Summer.

Seasons & Limits
As weather permits. Check Arizona and White Mountain Apache regulations for latest limits.

Accommodations & Services
All services available in Pinetop, Greer, and Sunrise.

Nearby Fly Fishing
Lots! The whole Fort Apache Reservation and eastern White Mountains have fly fishing stillwaters.

Rating
Depending on the day, a 5 or 6.

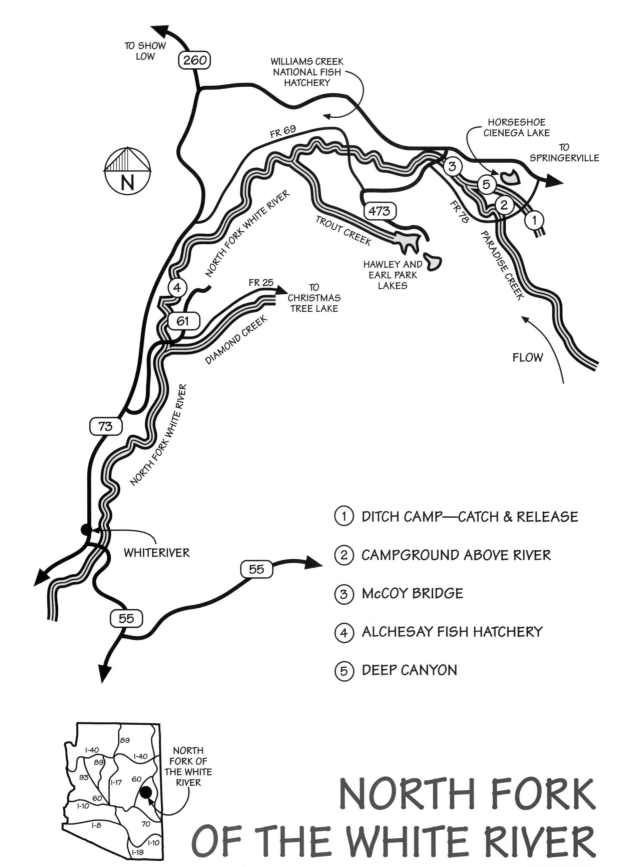

TO SHOW LOW
260

WILLIAMS CREEK NATIONAL FISH HATCHERY

FR 69

HORSESHOE CIENEGA LAKE

TO SPRINGERVILLE

N

NORTH FORK WHITE RIVER

TROUT CREEK

473

3

5

2

1

FR 78

PARADISE CREEK

HAWLEY AND EARL PARK LAKES

4

FR 25

TO CHRISTMAS TREE LAKE

61

DIAMOND CREEK

FLOW

73

NORTH FORK WHITE RIVER

WHITERIVER

55

55

(1) DITCH CAMP—CATCH & RELEASE

(2) CAMPGROUND ABOVE RIVER

(3) McCOY BRIDGE

(4) ALCHESAY FISH HATCHERY

(5) DEEP CANYON

89
I-40
I-40
89
93
I-17
60
60
I-10
I-8
70
I-10
I-19

NORTH FORK OF THE WHITE RIVER

NORTH FORK OF THE WHITE RIVER

NOT TO SCALE

North Fork of the White River

Anice-sized stream by Arizona standards, the North Fork of the White River begins on the west slope of Mt. Baldy and flows 25 miles to merge with the East Fork of the White, which forms the mainstem White River. From this point the White becomes too warm for good trout fishing.

This area is pristine and covered with thick pine, spruce, and willow trees. The water is clear and cold most of the year. Some of the upper stretches of this creek run through spectacular, ancient lava flows.

Before it meets the East Fork, the North Fork is a prime trout stream. It has a moderate gradient with lots of pools and riffles. There is a catch and release section at North Fork Ditch Camp, a well-known spot for lots of strong fish, including native Apache trout.

Healthy caddis and Baetis mayfly populations make for good dry fly fishing during the warmer months. When the fish won't rise, use a Beadhead Pheasant Tail or Hare's Ear tied below a large dry stonefly, or Hopper pattern. Then hang on. In the heat of summer into early fall, use a Hopper or large attractor dry for explosive results.

The North Fork of the White River is one of my favorite haunts, although poaching in the catch and release area is annoying. To reach this area from Pinetop, travel south on Hwy. 73 to the Log Road turnoff or stay on Hwy. 260 east of Hon Dah to the Hawley Lake turnoff. Cross the river and head west.

Types of Fish
Apache and brown trout.

Known Hatches
Golden and brown stoneflies, yellow sallys, caddis, mayflies, Baetis, PMDs, PEDs.

Equipment to Use
Rods: 4 weight, 6-½' to 8'.
Line: Floating double taper or weight forward.
Leaders: 4X–6X, 7-½'.
Wading: Chest-high waders and felt-soled boots or hip boots.

Flies to Use
Dries: #12–20 Adams, #16–20 BWO, #4–12 Turck's Tarantula, Hoppers, #4–12 Stimulators, Elk Hair Caddis.
Nymphs: #14–20 Gold Ribbed Hare's Ears #16–20, Pheasant Tail, #12–16 Caddis, #8–14 gold & brown Stonefly, #16–10 Yellow Sally. Carry all in beaded and nonbeaded.
Streamers: #6–8 black and brown Woolly Buggers.

When to Fish
Spring, summer, fall.

Seasons & Limits
Ditch Camp area is catch and release. The rest of the stream has the same regulations as other Apache Reservation streams. Consult the reservation regulations booklet.

Accommodations & Services
Sunrise Lake has a store, most other services available in Greer and Pinetop.

Nearby Fly Fishing
Little Colorado River, Sunrise Lake.

Rating
A solid 7 at Ditch Camp. The rest of the North Fork is a 6.

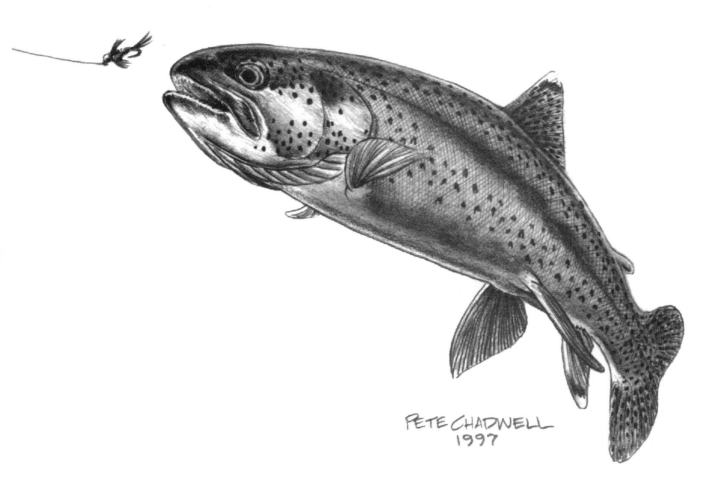

Rainbow Trout

Appendix

Arizona Fly Fishing Resources

AZ Fly Shops

Alta Vista Anglers
4730 N. 7th Ave.
Phoenix, AZ 85013
(602) 277-3111
www.altavistaanglers.com

AZ Flyfishing
31 W. Baseline Rd..
Tempe, AZ 85283
(480) 730-6808

Babbits
15 East Aspen Ave.
Flagstaff, AZ 86001
(928) 779-3253

Dry Creek Outfitters
5420 E. Broadway Blvd., Suite 254
Tucson, AZ 85711
(520) 326-7847
www.orvistucson.com

Lake Mary Fishing Boat Rentals
480 Lake Mary Rd.
Flagstaff, AZ 86001-9348
(928) 774-1742

Lake Patagonia Store
423 Lake Patagonia Rd.
Patagonia, AZ 85624
(520) 287-5545

Lynx Creek Unlimited
130 W. Gurly St., Ste. 307
Prescott, AZ 86301
(928) 776-7088

Mountain Outfitters
560 W. White Mountain Blvd.
Pinetop, AZ 85935
(928) 367-6200

On The Creek/Sedona Outfitters
274 Apple Ave., Suite C
Sedona, AZ 86336
(928) 203-9973

Orvis Scottsdale
7012 E. Greenway Pkwy.
Scottsdale, AZ 85254
(480) 905-1400

Paradise Creek Anglers
560 W. White Mountain Blvd.
Pinetop, AZ 85935
(928) 367-6200
www.paradisecreekanglers.com

Peace Surplus
14 W. Route 66
Flagstaff, AZ 86001
(928) 779-4521

Scottsdale Flyfishing company
10050 N. Scottsdale Rd., #101
Scottsdale, AZ 85253
(480) 368-9280
www.scottsdalefc.com

Tight Lines
4444 E. Grant Rd.., Ste.113
Tucson, AZ 85712
(520) 322-9444

Other Helpful Outfitters

Baja on the Fly
P.O. Box 81961
San Diego, CA 92138
(800) 919-2252
Mexico 011-52-114-82-1-79
www.bajafly.com

Durangler Flies & Supplies
923 Main Ave.
Durango, CO 81301
(970) 385-4081

High Desert Angler
435 S. Guadalupe
Santa Fe, NM 87501
(505) 98TROUT
www.highdesertangler.com

Los Pinos Fly Shop
3214 Matthew N.E.
Albuquerque, NM 87107
(800) 594-9637

Reel Life
1100 San Mateo, Ste. #60
Albuquerque, NM 87110
(505) 268-1693

Western Rivers Flyfisher
1071 East 900 S.
Salt Lake City, UT 84105
(800) 545-4312

Lees Ferry Accommodations

Marble Canyon Lodge
Rooms, restaurant, store, gas, and
other services.
(928) 355-2225

Cliff Dwellers Lodge
Rooms, food, and a gas station.
(928) 355-2228

Fly Fishing Organizations

AZ Flycasters
P.O. Box 44976
Phoenix, AZ 85064

Desert Flycasters
P.O. Box 41271
Mesa, AZ 85274-1271

Dame Juliana Anglers
P.O. Box 1727
Phoenix, AZ 85001-1727

Zane Grey Chapter
Trout Unlimited
4730 N. 7th Ave.
Phoenix, AZ 85013

Old Pueblo Chapter
Trout Unlimited
3542 W. Amber Terrace
Tucson, AZ 85741

Federation of Fly Fishers
National Headquarters
(800) 618-0808
Call for local club
www.fedflyfishers.org

International Game Fish Association
300 Gulf Stream Way
Dania Beach, FL 33004
(954) 927-2628

Government Resources

AZ Department of
Environmental Quality
3033 N. Central Ave., 3rd. Floor
Phoenix, AZ 85012

AZ Game and Fish Department
2221 W. Greenway Rd..
Phoenix, AZ 85023
(602) 942-3000
www.azgfd.com

U.S. Fish and Wildlife Service
(800) 275-3474

White Mountain Apache Wildlife and
Outdoor Recreation Division
P.O. Box 220
Whiteriver, AZ 85941
(928) 338-4385

Maps

Coconino National Forest
Tonto National Forest
Apache-Sitgreaves National Forest
Kaibab National Forest
National Forest Service
White Mountain Apache
Reservation Map
Earthshine
Lake Pleasant, Lees Ferry
Bartlett & Horseshoe Reservoirs
Roosevelt, Apache, Canyon,
Saguaro Lakes
Fish 'n Map Co.

The best source for maps of all kinds,
that I have ever seen is:
Wide World Of Maps (800) 279-7654
2626 W. Indian School Rd.
Phoenix, AZ 85017
(602) 279-2324
1444 W. Southern Ave.
Mesa, AZ 85202
(602) 279-2323

Recommended Reading

Fishing AZ,
G. J. Sagi

AZ Rivers and Stream Guide
AZ State Parks

Recreational Lakes of AZ
J. Reinhardt, et al.

The Black River Book: A Fishing &
Camping Guide
Earthshine

AZ Atlas & Gazetteer
DeLorme Mapping

The Baja Catch:
A Fishing & Camping Manual
for Baja California
Neil Kelly, Gene Kira

Mexico Blue Ribbon Fly Fishing
Ken Hanley

Guidebooks

www.amazon.com
www.bookzone.com
www.powells.com
www.justgoodbooks.com
www.barnesandnoble.com

Air Travel

American
www. aa.com
(800) 433-7300

America West
www.americawest.com
(800) 235-9292

Alaska
www.alaskaair.com
(800) 426-0333

Continental
www.continental.com
(800) 525-0280

Delta
www.delta.com
(800) 221-1212

Northwest
www.nwa.com
(800) 225-2525

Southwest
www.iflysw.com
(800) 435-9792

United
www.united.com
(800) 241-6522

USAirways
www. usair.com
(800) 428-4322

Travel Agents

www.itn.com
www.thetrip.com
www.travelweb.com
www.travelocity.com
www.expedia.com

Fly Fishing The Internet

www.flyshop.com
www.fbn-flyfish.com
www.flyfishamerica.com
www. gofishing.com
www.fly-fishing-women.com
www.tu.org
www.flyfishing.com.asf
www.ohwy.com
www.amrivers.org
http://gorp.away.com
www.gssafaris.com
www.flyfish.com

Directories

www.fish-world.com

No Nonsense Fly Fishing Knots

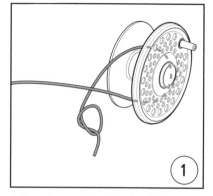
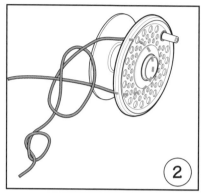
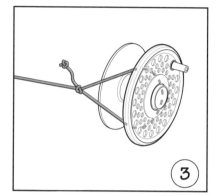

Arbot Knot—Use this simple knot to attach backing to your fly reel; 75 yards of backing will be plenty for most waters.

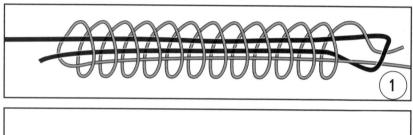
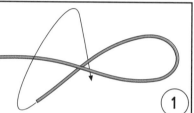

Blood Knot—Use this simple knot to connect sections of leader material. To add a Dropper, leave the heavier tag end long and attach fly.

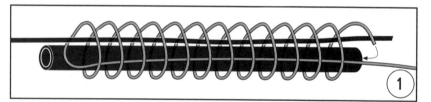

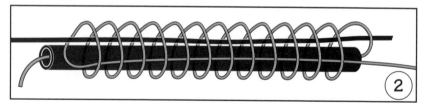

FLY LINE

LEADER

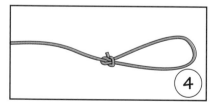

Nail Knot—Use a nail, needle, or small tube to tie this knot which connects the forward end of the fly line to the butt end of the leader. Follow this with a Perfection Loop, and you've got a permanent end loop that allows easy leader changes.

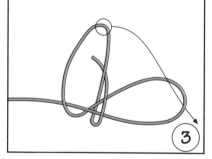

Perfection Loop—Use this knot to create a loop in the butt end of the leader. You can easily loop to loop your leader to your fly line.

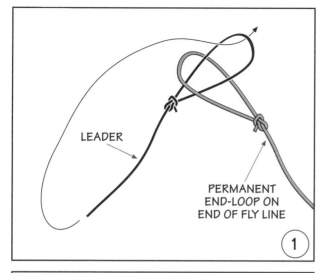

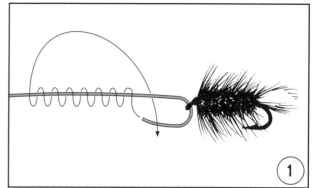

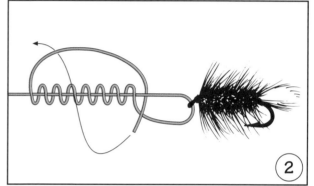

Loop to Loop—*Use this simple knot to connect the leader to an end loop on the tip of the fly line.*

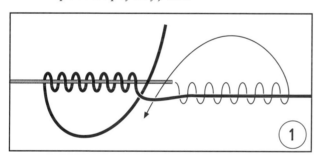

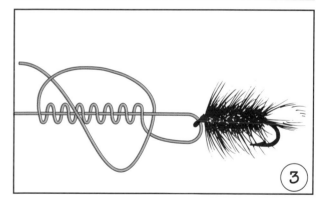

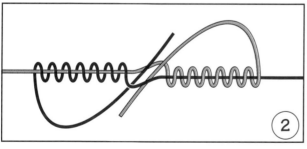

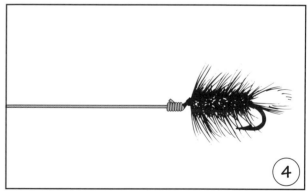

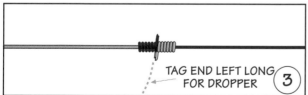

Blood Knot—*Use this simple knot to connect sections of leader material. To add a Dropper, leave the heavier tag end long and attach fly.*

Improved Clinch Knot—*Use this knot to attach a fly to the end of a tippet. Remember to moisten the knot just before you pull it tight.*

73

Find Your Way With These No Nonsense Guides

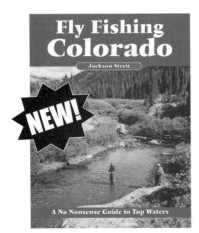

Fly Fishing Colorado

Jackson Streit

Your experienced guide gives you the quick, clear understanding of the essential information you'll need to fly fish Colorado's most outstanding waters. Use this book to plan your Colorado fly fishing trip, and take this guide along for ready reference. This popular guide has been updated, redesigned, and is in its third printing.

ISBN #1-892469-13-8......................$19.95

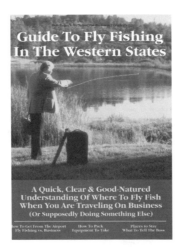

Business Traveler's Guide To Fly Fishing In The Western States

Bob Zeller

A seasoned road warrior reveals where one can fly fish within a two hour drive of every major airport in thirteen western states. Don't miss another day fishing!

ISBN #1-892469-01-4 ....$18.95

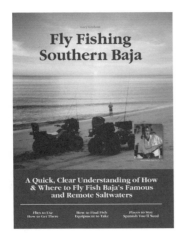

Fly Fishing Southern Baja

Gary Graham

With this book you can fly to Baja, rent a car and go out on your own to find exciting saltwater fly fishing! Mexico's Baja Peninsula is now one of the premier destinations for saltwater fly anglers.

ISBN #1-892469-00-6.....................$18.95

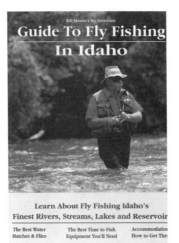

Fly Fishing Idaho

Bill Mason

The Henry's Fork, Salmon, Snake, and Silver Creek plus 24 other waters. Mr. Mason penned the first fly fishing guidebook to Idaho in 1994. It was updated in 1996 and showcases Bill's 30 plus years of Idaho fly fishing.

ISBN #0-9637256-1-0 ....$14.95

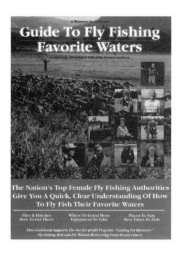

A Woman's Guide To
Fly Fishing Favorite Waters

Yvonne Graham

Forty-five of the top women fly fishing experts reveal their favorite waters. From scenic spring creeks in the East, big trout waters in the Rockies to exciting Baja; all described from the female perspective. A major donation goes to Casting for Recovery, a nonprofit organization for women recovering from breast cancer.

ISBN #1-892469-03-0 ... $19.95

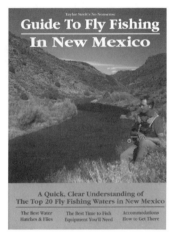

Fly Fishing New Mexico

Taylor Streit

Since 1970, Mr. Streit has been New Mexico's *foremost* fly fishing authority and professional guide. He's developed many fly patterns used throughout the region. Taylor owned the Taos Fly Shop for ten years and managed a bone fishing lodge in the Bahamas. He makes winter fly fishing pilgrimages to Argentina where he escorts fly fishers and explorers.

ISBN #1-892469-04-9 ....$18.95

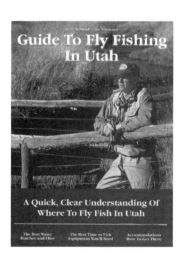

Fly Fishing Utah

Steve Schmidt

Utah yields extraordinary, uncrowded and little known fishing. Steve Schmidt, outfitter and owner of Western Rivers Fly Shop in Salt Lake City has explored these waters for over 28 years. Fly fishing mountain streams and lakes, tailwaters, bass waters and reservoirs.

ISBN #0-9637256-8-8 ....$19.95

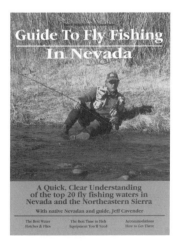

Fly Fishing Pyramid Lake Nevada

Terry Barron

The Gem of the Desert is full of huge Lahontan cutthroat trout. Terry has recorded everything you need to fly fish the most outstanding trophy cutthroat fishery in the U.S. Where else can you get tired of catching 18-25" trout?

ISBN #0-9637256-3-7 ....$15.95

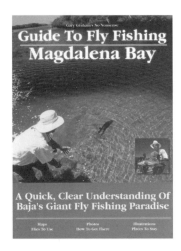

Fly Fishing Magdalena Bay
Gary Graham

Guide and excursion leader Gary Graham (Baja On The Fly) lays out the truth about fly fishing for snook in mangroves, off-shore marlin, calving whales from Alaska, beautiful birds, kayaking, even surfing. Photos, illustrations, maps, and travel information, this is "the Bible" for this unique region.

ISBN #1-892469-08-1 ....$24.95

Seasons of the Metolius
John Judy

This new book describes how a beautiful riparian environment both changes and stays the same over the years. This look at nature comes from a man who makes his living working in nature and chronicles John Judy's 30 years of study, writing and fly fishing his beloved home water, the crystal clear Metolius River in central Oregon.

ISBN #1-892469-11-1 ....$21.95

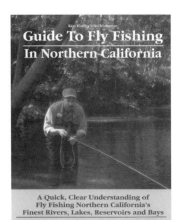

Fly Fishing Northern California
Ken Hanley

Coming Soon: Mr. Hanley and some very talented contributors like Jeff Solis, Dave Stanley, Katie Howe and others, have fly fished nearly every top water in California. Saltwater, bass, steelhead, high mountains, they provide all you need to discover the best places to fly fish in the Golden State.

ISBN #1-892469-10-3 ....$19.95

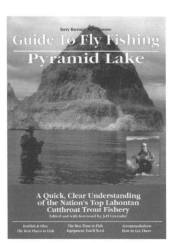

Fly Fishing Nevada
Dave Stanley

The Truckee, Walker, Carson, Eagle, Davis, Ruby, mountain lakes, and more. Mr. Stanley is recognized nationwide as the most knowledgeable fly fisher and outdoorsman in the stae of Nevada. He owns and operates the Reno Fly Shop and Truckee River Outfitters in Truckee, California.

ISBN #0-9637256-3-9 ....$18.95

Fly Fishing Lee's Ferry

Dave Foster

This colorful guide provides a clear understanding of the complex and fascinating 15 miles of river that can provide fly anglers 40-fish days. Detailed maps direct fly and spin fishing access. Learn history, boating and geology and see the area's beauty. Indispensable for the angler and intrepid visitor to the Marble Canyon.

ISBN #1-892469-07-3......................$21.95

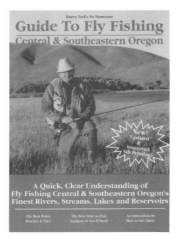

Fly Fishing Central and Southeastern Oregon

Harry Teel

Coming Soon: The Metolius, Deschutes, McKenzie, Owyhee, John Day and 35 other waters. Mr. Teel's 60 years of fly fishing went into the first No Nonsense fly fishing guide, published in 1993 and updated, expanded and improved in 1998 by Jeff Perin. Now updated again and bigger and better than ever.

ISBN #1-892469-09-X....................$19.95

Where No Nonsense Guides Come From

No Nonsense guidebooks give you a quick, clear, understanding of the essential information needed to fly fish a region's most outstanding waters. The authors are highly experienced and qualified local fly fishers. Maps are tidy versions of the authors sketches.

These guides are produced by the fly fishers, their friends, and spouses of fly fishers, at No Nonsense Fly Fishing Guidebooks. The publisher is located in Tucson, Arizona.

All who produce No Nonsense guides believe in providing top quality products at a reasonable price. We also believe all information should be verified. We never hesitate to go out, fly rod in hand, to verify the facts and figures that appear in the pages of these guides. The staff is committed to this research. It's dirty work, but we're glad to do it for you.

Author Glenn Tinnin with a nice rainbow at mile 7.5 on Lees Ferry. Scott Baxter Photo.

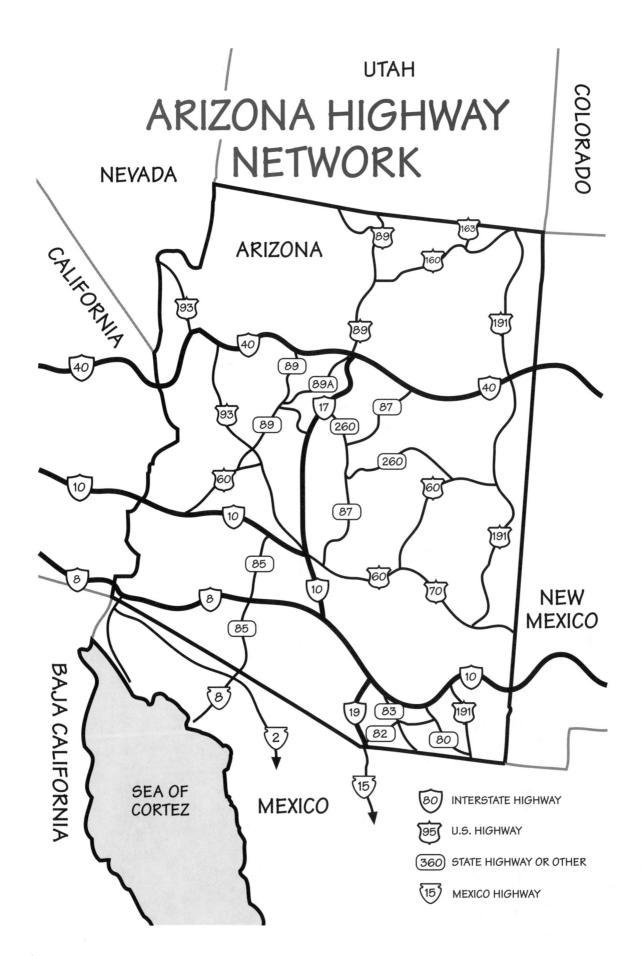

ARIZONA HIGHWAY NETWORK

UTAH

COLORADO

NEVADA

CALIFORNIA

ARIZONA

NEW MEXICO

BAJA CALIFORNIA

SEA OF CORTEZ

MEXICO

80 INTERSTATE HIGHWAY

95 U.S. HIGHWAY

360 STATE HIGHWAY OR OTHER

15 MEXICO HIGHWAY